W9-CSG-848

SERIOUS CYCLING
FOR THE BEGINNER

SERIOUS CYCLING FOR THE BEGINNER

by Ray Adams

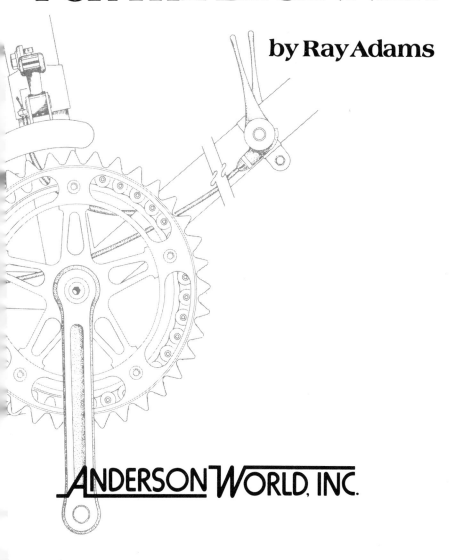

ANDERSON WORLD, INC.

Contents

Foreword

When I bought my first bicycle, I didn't even know how to shift the gears. The man who sold it to me gave me such a poor explanation of shifting that I wound up owning a 10-speed bicycle without having any idea of how to use it. I couldn't shift gears, and I didn't know how to get on and off that high saddle.

So I went out and bought a book. The book told me how everything worked, including the gears. Armed with my new knowledge, I went out and tried my new bicycle. That's when I found out that there were a hundred things the book didn't mention. (Neither did the next 20 books I bought.)

This volume was not meant to be a book in the traditional sense. It was written as a training manual and a guide for those who have purchased a new 10-speed bicycle, and know very little about this sophisticated machine. *Serious Cycling for the Beginner* is useful even if you have ridden other types of bicycles. If the last bicycle you rode was a single-gear balloon-tire bicycle, you'll soon realize that a 10-speed bicycle is as different from a one-speed as a high-strung race horse is from an old gray mare.

There are more benefits to cycling than helping reduce pollution, traffic congestion, etc. Cycling reawakens your confidence to depend on your mind, spirit and body. It helps you to see the world around you with a freshness that you thought you had lost.

In short, it helps you to get to know yourself better, to like yourself more and to be proud of yourself as a human being. I don't really see where any of us can ask for much more than that.

Benefits of Cycling

Cycling is truly a unique sport. No other activity that we engage in "just for the fun of it" provides so many physical, mental and emotional bonuses whether we seek them or not.

These free bonuses have become increasingly important. Every year more Americans find themselves working at jobs that require less physical activity, placing them under greater mental and emotional stress. In addition, we find ourselves bombarded on all sides with advertisements urging us to eat more, smoke more, drink more. As we age, we get out of shape, become overweight and eventually lapse into a state where we never seem to feel good. After awhile, this lack of physical fitness affects our mental health and emotional outlook.

Millions of persons just give up and go along with this gradual deterioration. There is no reason they should weigh 40 pounds more than they did at age 20 and have to gasp their way up a flight of stairs or feel exhausted after walking a mile.

American closets and garages are cluttered with books, gadgets, exercisers, pills, weights and similar items purchased in an effort to lose weight and feel good again. The reason for this confusion is that many Americans are unaware of the numerous pleasures that bicycling has to offer.

EXERCISE OR ENJOYMENT?

The key word is *exercise*. No matter how we try to get around it, we tend to think of exercise as a chore, an unpleasant task that we must perform in order to improve our health.

There is another word that goes with exercise: that's *regular*. In order for exercise to be of any value, it must be performed on a regular basis. Irregular attempts at exercising are not only useless, but also a waste of time.

Most of us have tried an exercise program at one time or another for one, maybe two weeks. However, the whole thing gets to be such a bore that we start looking for things to do that are more important than daily exercise. All we are left with is a bitter taste in our mouths at having tried something and failed.

It is true that many beginning cyclists over the age of 25 take up bicycling for the exercise. However, they soon forget about exercise and start enjoying themselves. They get their exercise as a free bonus. Bonus or not, these benefits are real and tangible, and we should take a little time to consider their value. Here are some of the benefits you'll receive.

HEALTH BENEFITS

Heart disease is by far the leading cause of death in the United States. No definitive study proves that the active individual suffers fewer heart attacks than the inactive one. Nevertheless, most medical authorities feel that a regular program of exercise is beneficial.

As the late Dr. Paul Dudley White, a noted cardiologist, stated, "I would like to put everybody on bicycles. Not once in awhile but as a regular routine. That's a good way to prevent heart disease." In addition, he felt that bicycling aided the lungs. Carried out under supervised conditions, cycling has helped to alleviate emphysema, silicosis and tuberculosis.

If the American government were to name one problem as our national disease, it would probably be obesity. There is no other health problem that so many Americans of all ages struggle with. Each year we spend billions of dollars and millions of hours struggling with diets, pills and other reducing aids. Everyone looks for the magic formula that will make the unwanted pounds disappear, but there is no magic formula. The only way to reduce is to eat less.

However, bicycling can help keep your weight down. Regular bicycling uses up some of those calories that turn into fat. The individual who engages in a regular riding program can — and needs to — consume more calories than the individual who does not exercise.

The effect of cycling on stress is more direct. Stress is both a mental and a physical problem. Because of the mental and emotional pressures we build up during the day, we often suffer from high blood pressure, ulcers and nerves.

In addition, cycling's effect on relieving stress is remarkable. A vigorous 30- to 60-minute ride after a bad day at the office has the same relaxing effect as gulping down three double martinis. And the effects on your body and mind are considerably better. A long ride on a weekend cleanses your mind and body of the week's accumulated poisons.

One of the best moments of the day happens after you arrive home from your evening ride. The tensions you brought home from work are gone. You feel relaxed and at ease, discovering that you like your own body and feeling a bit proud of it. You feel good.

Cycling even has an effect on cigarette smoking. Those individuals who stop smoking after they have taken up cycling will find that their lungs feel larger, cleaner and don't hurt as much. Best of all, as their cycling improves they soon discover that smoking hinders their riding endurance. This provides an extra incentive to stop smoking.

INCREASED STRENGTH AND ENDURANCE

A well-planned cycling program also helps reduce back troubles. Better yet, it may prevent them. As your strength increases, your posture improves.

Strength also increases in your legs, and you don't have to worry about your legs turning into masses of muscular knots. My own legs have always been rather bulky. However, I discovered that they actually got slimmer as they grew stronger.

Your endurance will increase enormously. When you begin riding, you may discover that you get tired almost as soon as you begin. After a summer of regular cycling, you are able to sustain a high level of activity that was only a dream a few months before.

These increases in strength and endurance can have useful side effects. Every year I use a 12-foot pole with a saw on one end to cut branches off the trees in my yard. Before I began cycling I had to stop and rest every few minutes when pruning my trees. Now I can work steadily for half an hour and still not feel tired.

OTHER BENEFITS

I have found other benefits in cycling, some of which are rarely mentioned. As we grow older and more sedentary, our coordination declines. None of us will ever be what we were at 20, but cycling helps us regain some of that coordination we have lost. As our reflexes improve, we move more easily, quickly and gracefully.

There is no need to stick to any special diet in order to enjoy cycling. Yet most of us begin paying more attention to what we eat. We start cutting out the junk foods, and concentrate on eating good nutritional foods that provide the necessary fuel for strenuous workouts. For the chronically overweight, this can be a real bonus.

Cycling is an ideal form of exercise that is beneficial to individuals of all ages. It allows us to control the rate and intensity at which we exercise. A cyclist can begin as slowly as desired, taking all the time needed to warm up and maintain the same rate of exercise for any desired length of time and then taper off or quit.

One of the important rides offered by bicycle clubs is the "Century." A Century is a ride of 100 miles and must be completed in one day. It is somewhat similar to the runner's marathon. More often than not, the most enthusiastic Century cyclists are people who have retired and are in their 60s, 70s and 80s.

The mental/emotional rewards of cycling can be as great as the physical ones. From almost the first ride, the beginning cyclist learns to monitor and evaluate the condition of his or her body. This is the time many of us discover that we have no idea what condition our body is in. We have become strangers to our bodies.

A most spectacular change will occur when you get out of your car and onto a bicycle. For the first time you'll realize how isolated you've become from the real world when riding around in an automobile. Suddenly, you realize that you are venturing through the real world instead of racing past it. You become aware of the trees, the smell of grass, people talking on their lawn. You notice, perhaps for the first time, that the streets you've been driving over for years are not flat, but undulating, even hilly. You also discover there is something known as the wind, and that it flows in regular, unpredictable patterns. If you are the type that likes to explore, you will learn more about your city in one year riding a bicycle than in 15 years of driving a car.

Cycling is an activity that can accommodate any temperament. Riding clubs provide a social atmosphere for the cyclist who likes to ride with others. In addition, cycling with close friends or members of one's family also provides emotional benefits for all. Furthermore, bicycling is an excellent pastime for the solitary person who prefers riding alone. The housewife can get away for a while and be herself and belong to herself, alone with her bicycle.

ESTABLISHING A PROGRAM

Cycling is still a strenuous exercise, although you never think of it when you begin to enjoy riding. The prudent individual who is overweight and out of condition will follow these steps before beginning to ride:

● Get a physical checkup. It is good sense to get a thorough physical checkup before engaging in a strenuous program. When you are learning to ride a 10-speed bicycle, you are engaging in a strenuous activity. When you get your checkup, tell your doctor that you plan to take up bicycling, and follow his advice.

● Engage in a gradually accelerating exercise program before you begin to ride. You should begin with some form of moderate physical training, because there are lower limits to the amount of energy you can put out and still make a bicycle move. The sudden demands of bicycle riding after months or years of relative inactivity can be harmful.

Progressively longer walks is a good start. These can be followed by jogging or uphill hikes or something similar. This program should have your doctor's approval.

I don't exercise anymore. I ride a bicycle for the fun of it.

The fact that I am getting the exercise anyway has become a free gift instead of an unpleasant duty. How many other physical fitness programs can say that?

Spend two weeks walking on level ground before you start hiking uphill. Then hike to the top of the trail in progressively longer stages.

Serious Cycling for the Beginner

Buying Your 10-Speed Bicycle

Bicycles look alike to the untrained eye. Yet two apparently identical machines can be as different as a Volkswagen and a Ferrari. Purchasing the right bicycle for your needs can make cycling a pleasure, whereas purchasing the wrong one can doom your cycling efforts before they begin.

SELECTING YOUR BIKE

Buy your bicycle at a bicycle shop. *Never* buy it from a large department store or from any place that sells bicycles as a sideline. Most department store bicycles are poor quality merchandise. And more often than not, the salesperson knows little or nothing about bicycles. He or she may have been selling electric toasters for some time.

Although the bicycles on exhibit in such stores are assembled, the one you receive is usually still boxed and only partially assembled. It can take an experienced cyclist six to eight hours to put it together. Some stores will assemble the bicycle for you (for a fee), but the work is seldom first class. If your bicycle breaks down and you take it back to the store, you may have to wait weeks for the parts to arrive.

A good bicycle shop will have knowledgeable salespeople to wait on you, and your bicycle will be fully and expertly assembled at no charge. A reputable shop will ask you to bring it back in 30 to 90 days for a free checkup. If a part breaks down, they will have a replacement in stock.

Visit as many bicycle shops as you can before making a

purchase. Talk to the salespeople, and tell them that you know nothing about bicycles. Ask the salesperson to explain terms you do not understand. Do business with the shop that seems most experienced, and not with the one most conveniently located.

When you are buying your first bicycle, the most valuable aid you can have is an experienced salesperson to deal with. If you can find one who is truly first rate, you really don't need anything else to aid you in your bicycle selection.

PRICE RANGE

In bicycles, like anything else, you get what you pay for. Unless you are very experienced and very lucky, you are not likely to get a good new 10-speed bicycle today for less than $125. I know that you've seen glowing ads offering "racing" bicycles for $79.95. Don't believe them. A decent bicycle will cost a decent price. A top price to pay for a good general purpose bicycle would be about $250.00.

There are several types of bicycles. Trying to use certain words to describe them can be tricky. This is because advertisers use all kinds of terms in their efforts to make their particular kind of bicycle more attractive. A general purpose bicycle, for example, is often called a touring bicycle. In this case, the term "touring" is at once true and misleading. You can ride across the United States on a good general purpose bicycle. Thousands of people have done it. So you could call it a touring bicycle. On the other hand, a general purpose bicycle is not specifically designed for long-distance touring.

Don't be misled by the term "racing" when applied to a bicycle. While there may be an exception or two, true racing bicycles start at about $400.

BIKE WEIGHT RECOMMENDATIONS

A bicycle's weight is not an absolute guide to its quality. However, it does provide a good indication of a bicycle's quality and construction. Ten-speed bicycles weighing more than 42 pounds are usually of poor quality. Try to avoid them. Remember, you have to move your bicycle forward with your own energy.

A good bicycle in the price range already mentioned should weigh between 25 and 36 pounds. The closer to 25 pounds the better. If possible, try to get one weighing 32 pounds or less.

Oddly enough, in this price range you should be wary of any bicycle weighing much less than 24 or 25 pounds. Overall sturdiness may have been sacrificed in an effort to reduce the total weight.

WHAT TO LOOK FOR

When discussing a bicycle, the salesperson will be using terms that may be unfamiliar to you. There are at least three terms that you should understand: derailleurs, double-butted and lugs. Ask the salesperson to explain them carefully.

Derailleurs are devices which "derail" the bicycle chain from one set of gears to another set. A 10-speed bicycle has two derailleurs. Ask the salesperson to point them out and to demonstrate how they work.

The term double-butted refers to the type of tubing used to make the bicycle frame. The frame tubes don't have to be as strong in the middle as on the ends. A butted piece of frame tubing is thicker at the end of the tube than in the middle. A double-butted tube is thicker on both ends and thinner in the middle. This change of thickness occurs on the inside of the tube. Using this kind of tubing instead of straight gauge tubing saves weight. It also costs more money.

There is one important point to remember. Just because one tube in the frame is double-butted does not mean that all tubes are. A bicycle where all tubing is double-butted can be quite expensive.

Look for lugs at the joints of the bicycle frame. In a way, a lug looks somewhat like those plumbing fittings known as tees and elbows. They are of course much lighter, thinner and more attractive. Lugs are used on good bicycles at the joints instead of weldings, because welding temperatures tend to weaken the metal of the tubing.

Brake Lever
Turned Down Handlebars
Head Tube
Front Fork
Spoke
Wheel Hub
Tire
Chainwheels
Stem
Gear Levers
Top Tube
Seat Tube
Down Tube
Crank
Pedal
Toe Strap
Toe Clip
Saddle
Seat Post
Front Derailleur
Caliper Brakes
Chain Stay
Seat Stay
Tire Rim
Tire
Freewheel, or Rear Sprocket Cluster
Rear Derailleur
Tire Valve
Chain

10—SPEED BICYCLE

DETERMINING BIKE SIZES

A bicycle's size isn't measured from the ground up, because it is possible to make a bicycle taller or shorter by using different sized tires. Its size is determined by measuring the frame from the center of the bottom bracket spindle to the center of the top tube, along the seat tube.

Bicycle sizes run from approximately 19 to 26 inches. A 19-inch bicycle might be the right size for someone five feet tall. A 26-inch bicycle would be needed for someone 6 feet, 4 inches or taller. I am 5 feet, 10 inches tall. I can use a 22½- or 23-inch bicycle.

Here is how you determine your bicycle size. Wear a pair of shoes with reasonably thin soles when going to the bicycle shop. When checking a bicycle, straddle it and place *both* feet flat on the floor. There should be a minimum of a 1/2- to 3/4-inch clearance between the crotch and the top tube of the bicycle. Never buy a bicycle you cannot straddle in this way.

Even if you cannot yet ride your bicycle, it is a good idea to try sitting on it in order to make sure that the seat is the right height. Have the salesperson hold the bicycle while you get up on the seat. Place the ball of your foot on one of the pedals and push the pedal all the way down. Let the salesperson adjust the seat up or down to suit you.

HANDLEBARS AND SADDLE

Purchase a bicycle with turned-down or "Maes" handlebars. Much of the effectiveness of a good 10-speed bicycle is lost when you use the regular upright handlebars.

One of the things that bothers many people buying their first bicycle is that small seat, or saddle, as it is usually called. Buy your bicycle with one of the smaller saddles. You won't like it at first, but you will get used to it. It has definite advantages over the larger, springier models.

If you are a woman, you should try to get a saddle designed specifically for women cyclists. This may not be easy to do. It is only recently that the bicycling industry has realized that a woman needs a different shaped saddle than a man. Look around until you find one. If the bicycle shop where you want to purchase your bicycle does not have such a saddle, it will be worth your time to shop around until you find one.

GEAR RECOMMENDATION

You should make sure that your bicycle has the proper gearing system for your part of the country. If you live in very flat country, a low gear of 40 to 50 inches should be sufficient. However, if there are any hills in your area, insist on a gearing system where the low gear is 40 inches or even lower. As a beginner, you will never make it up a steep hill in a 50-inch gear.

Chapter six provides additional information that will assist you in understanding gear systems, and help you make the proper choice when selecting your 10-speed bicycle.

3
Learning to Ride

Public streets are not the proper place for your first lesson on a 10-speed bicycle. This holds true even if you rode the old one-speed bicycle once before. If you live in a city of any size, there are a surprising number of places available for your first riding sessions.

Your practice area should be hard-surfaced with as few cracks, bumps and potholes as possible. It should also be available to you at a time when it is empty.

The size of the area is also important, since a 10-speed bicycle moves faster than you think. The best areas are parking lots for football stadiums, sports arenas, race tracks and gymnasiums. If no such area is available, and you must use a street, find a fairly deserted one, preferably a dead end.

If you *must* practice on a street, use a deserted industrial street during weekends.

PROPER STARTING GEAR

The first thing to do before leaving home is to make sure that your bicycle is in the proper gear. You can begin to ride with the bicycle set in any one of the 10 gears. However, if your bike is in an extremely high or low gear, starting can be difficult.

Generally, the middle gears are the best to start pedalling with. This means that the bicycle chain should go around the larger of the two front sprockets (often called chainwheels) and around the second largest sprocket of the rear wheel. This will usually put the bike in fifth gear. Most bike shops will set your bike at or around that gear when you purchase it. If it's not set at this gear follow this procedure:

● Turn your bicycle upside down so it sits by itself.

● There are two levers attached to the down tube at the forward section of the bicycle. A small cable leads away from each of these levers. Follow the cable that goes to the long mechanism (rear derailleur) next to the rear sprockets. This derailleur shifts gears on the rear wheel. The other lever moves the front derailleur, which shifts the bicycle chain back and forth between the two front chainwheels. Never move either of these two gear levers unless the pedals and rear wheel are turning forward.

● Assume that the bicycle chain is on the wrong gear both front and back. Let's take a look at the rear gears first. Remember, you want to get the chain to go around the second largest rear sprocket. Turn the pedals forward by hand, making sure the rear wheel is turning. Now, gently move the gear lever for the rear sprockets. The bicycle chain will begin to move from one rear sprocket to another. Keep moving the lever until the chain is on the second largest sprocket.

You find the right direction for lever to move

● Do the same for the front sprocket, changing the chain to the larger, outside chainwheel by moving the other gear shifting lever. Notice that the front guide will move the chain to the right or left. Move the lever until the guide moves away from the chain, and the chattering noise stops. Don't push the control lever too far or you'll change gears and have to repeat the gear-changing process.

Serious Cycling for the Beginner

• If the chain is rubbing between the sprockets on the rear wheel, adjust the left control lever until the chain runs easily into the second largest rear sprocket. Your bicycle is now ready to ride.

GETTING STARTED

Getting started can be trickier than it seems. First, stand on the left side of the bike and adjust the pedal to the 10 o'clock position. Put your left foot on the pedal and push down on it firmly. This movement allows you to lift yourself up, back and down onto the saddle. Press down on the right pedal and you're on your way.

Once you've started, circle your wide practice area for awhile, making wide turns and building your self-confidence. As you progress you'll be able to do figure 8s.

USING YOUR BRAKES

You should get into the habit of always using both brakes at the same time. The first time you use the brakes, press them gently. Jamming them too suddenly will teach you another method of stopping known as "going over the handlebars." As you near the point where the bicycle is going to come to a stop, apply slightly more pressure until the bike has completely stopped.

There's no need to raise yourself off the saddle at this point of your bicycling development. If the bicycle leans to the right, put your right foot out and let the bicycle lean until your right foot touches ground. On the other hand, if the bicycle leans to the left, put your weight on the saddle and not on your left foot.

With practice, you can come out of the saddle cleanly and easily, and touch down with your right foot while the bicycle is straight up.

HOLDING THE HANDLEBARS

Initially, you'll discover that it is extremely difficult to remove one hand from the handlebars. If you remove your left hand, for example, the front wheel may veer sharply to the left, forcing you to make a frantic grab for the handlebars.

The proper way of learning to ride with one hand is to

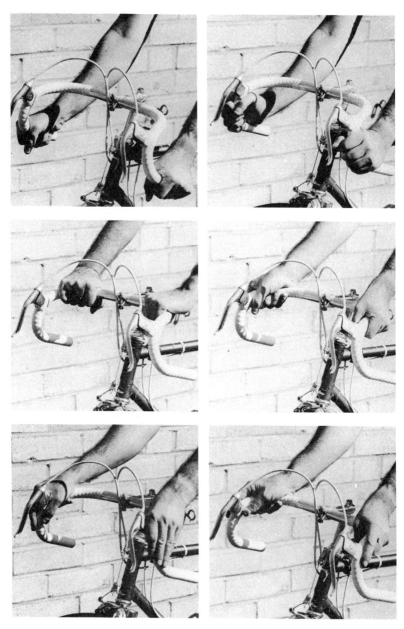

Some of the most common hand positions are shown above. Experiment with these positions, and discover others which best suit your needs.

Serious Cycling for the Beginner

support your weight with your stomach and back muscles just before you remove one hand from the bars. This takes the pressure off the hand remaining on the bicycle. Riding with one hand is one of the few things you won't have to consciously practice.

How do you manage to take one hand off the handlebars to shift gears? Place your right hand over the center of the handlebars with the stem under the palm of your hand. Take your left hand off the handlebars. The bicycle will probably wobble, but you should be able to continue.

You will be shifting gears as you progress. Learning to reach down to the gear control levers provides enough practice. Eventually, you'll casually and easily reach for a lever or adjust your hat with one hand without moving the other.

FEET AND PEDALS

No other part of your body will have to master as many new physical skills as your legs and feet. From the start, pedal with the ball of the foot on the center of the pedals, and don't use the heel or the arch of your foot. It should be evident at once that using the ball of the foot is the most effective method of pushing down on the pedals.

Try to maintain a good, moderate speed. If your legs begin to hurt, or your breathing becomes labored, slow down. Whatever you do, stop before you get too tired. Waiting until you are exhausted can cause pain to your legs. Stop and rest when you feel a little weak, and quit altogether when you get tired.

REFINING YOUR SKILLS

Pick a spot in your practice area where you want to stop. It can be a leaf, a scrap of paper or a line printed on the riding surface. Aim for it, and stop as close as you can to that mark. Don't slam on the brakes if you are going to overshoot your mark, or you may have a nasty fall.

You can also practice turning. On the first day about all you could handle were wide, slow turns. Now try tightening up the turn a little, by consciously leaning into the turn. Eventually, you'll learn to do this unconsciously, but for now make a definite effort to think about leaning when you turn.

Above is an ideal practice area. It has plenty of space, islands and white lines to practice your steering, turning and braking skills.

It's important to practice your technique before you venture out to the street. You want to develop a respectable turn without conscious effort.

Get into the habit of not using your brakes while turning. Later on, under more difficult conditions, braking while negotiating a curve can be hazardous.

If you're in a parking lot, look around to see if there is a long, straight line painted on the surface. Guide the bicycle along the line, pedalling the bike as straight as possible. One of the irritations of these first days arises from watching others ride in a straight line with a steady front wheel. With some practice and confidence, you'll soon be able to do the same.

Also practice Ss and figure 8s, and make tighter turns than the first day.

Up to now, you've been riding as far away as possible from

Serious Cycling for the Beginner

anything you could hit. However, you won't be staying away from traffic for long. Every bicycle rider must learn to ride with the street curb close to his bicycle. If the parking lot has any kind of a curb, move over to it and ride beside it. On your first attempts, get three or four feet away and ride parallel to the curb. Then move closer as you gain confidence. Riding close to the curb was one of the hardest things for me to learn. This was true on my first series of street trips as well as my rides on the practice area. For a while I was almost convinced that there was some magnetic attraction between the curb and the front wheel of my bicycle.

Let's say that you are riding down the street close to the right curb. Suddenly the bicycle veers toward the curb. Your natural reaction is to whip the wheel to the left. That's where a dangerous situation can occur. If you whip the wheel too hard to the left you may suddenly find that you have steered into the middle of the auto lane. If there is an automobile approaching from behind, you could be hit or cause an accident. You usually won't get an opportunity to use your brakes in such situations. The chances are that you won't have time to reach down for the brakes. So think about this situation before you get into it, and try to decide what you will do before it occurs.

MAINTAIN A STEADY CADENCE

Learning to pedal your bicycle at the same steady rate as much of the time as possible is an important skill. Cadence is something you must begin to acquire a feel for as soon as possible, for you will never be an efficient cyclist until you do.

Maintaining cadence is a more difficult task than you might realize. Pedalling at the same steady rate is easy enough when you actually think about it. However, as soon as you concentrate on something else, your pedalling rate tends to become erratic. It takes a while to get to the point where you always pedal at the same rate automatically.

Your ability to use the gears of your 10-speed bicycle greatly affects the maintenance of a steady cadence. No one masters one of these skills without mastering the other. If you're pedalling at 70 rpm on the flat and come to a slight rise, you won't be able to continue at that rate. Only a gear change will help.

GEAR SHIFTING

no pressure

The gears are the heart of the 10-speed bicycle. Learning to use them is the most difficult of all skills you will have to learn.

The seasoned cyclist will tell you that it is too soon in your training to start using the gear system on your bicycle and will recommend that you ride at least 50 or 60 miles before you start shifting gears.

I agree with this, but I also know that you have no intention of waiting that long. The person who purchases a 10-speed bicycle for the first time is usually itching to try out the gears. I would have tried them out myself on the very first day if I could. However, every time I took my hand off the handlebars to reach for a lever the front wheel started to wobble, forcing me to wait until my second practice session.

Usually, on a 10-speed bicycle, the left lever controls the front gears, and the right lever controls the rear gears. If you have any doubts about your own bicycle, simply look at the gears and follow the cable leading down from the lever, and notice which gear it goes to. I used to keep saying, "Right-rear! Right-rear!" to myself until I got used to the gears.

There are at least two things you should know before you begin:

• Never change the gear levers unless your bicycle is in motion, and the pedals are turning. Also, never stop your bicycle until a gear shift has been completed. Doing either of these can cause the chain to become caught and break some of the gear teeth or bend the front or rear derailleur. A more complete discussion of this can be found in chapter six.

friction shifters

• There is no way to memorize the exact position of the lever in order to put the bicycle into a certain gear. The gear shift levers are connected to the gears by a thin cable, and these cables can stretch.

To begin, get your bicycle moving into an area where you have a lot of open space ahead of you, and pedal at a moderate rate of speed. Move the left lever which controls the front gears.

You will hear a rattling sound as the chain moves from one sprocket to the other on the chainwheel. If the chain has moved from the larger sprocket to the smaller one, you will quickly find it easier to pedal. If you continue to pedal at the same rate, you'll begin to slow down. Shifting the chain from the smaller sprocket to the larger one makes pedalling harder at low speeds.

If you shift gears perfectly, there should be no sound coming from the front gears. However, if you hear a slight chattering sound, move the left lever back just slightly, in the direction you moved it from, until the chattering disappears. If you don't make this minor adjustment, the chain will continue to rattle against the front derailleur and bend it out of shape. Eventually, the front derailleur will be unable to transfer the chain properly from one front sprocket to the other. Train your ears to listen for this chattering, and make the proper gear lever adjustment when the noise occurs. Now move the right lever. You will need a more delicate touch here than on the gear shift lever for the front sprockets. Both levers can move about the same distance, but the range of movement on the front lever controls only one gear change. On the rear one you can move into any one of five gears. So move the right gear lever more slowly than you moved the left one. Practice going from one gear to another, while continuing to pedal at the same rate. By doing this, you get a better idea of the effect of the gear change.

One thing to remember. Any time the chain seems to get caught or stuck, stop at once and see what is the matter. Never pedal in the hope that if you pedal hard enough, the chain will come loose. You will only succeed in jamming the chain so tightly that it will take you forever to loosen it.

POST LESSON CHECKS

Once the lesson is over, you should take your bicycle home and check it. Turn the bicycle upside down. (Whenever you have to change a tire this is usually the best position to have the bicycle.)

When doing anything else with your bicycle, it is usually a better idea to hang the bicycle upright from the ceiling of your garage. Attach two hooks or eye screws from the ceiling about six feet apart. Hang a rope from each with a hook at the end to support your bicycle.

Once you have the bicycle hanging, you might make a few simple checks. Spin the wheels to see if the rubber brake pads are rubbing against the rims. Brakes are attached to the frame by one bolt and can move to the right or left. As a result, one of the brake pads may touch the wheels even when the brakes are not being used. If one brake pad is touching, then tap the brakes on one side until they are centered again.

The main reason you've suspended your bicycle is to make a clear examination of the gears.

While shifting the gears back and forth, turn the pedals at the same rate of speed. In this way you can easily see the results of making gear changes.

Notice the derailleur attached to the dropout where the seat-stay meets the chainstay. It moves the chain, derailling it from one sprocket to another.

While practicing with the front derailleur, shift the chain from one sprocket to another, pushing the gear lever as far as it will go. If this small, rectangular guide is rubbing against the chain and making a chattering sound, move the lever back a bit. The front derailleur will move away from the chain, and the chattering will stop.

You may find that when you shift gears in the front, the chattering is occurring in the rear. If this is so, adjust the rear derailleur.

When you shift the chain from the smaller front sprocket to the larger one, the rear wheel turns faster. However, it also takes more effort to pedal at the same rate in this higher gear.

It's just the opposite on the rear gears. On the rear, the smallest sprocket is the highest gear and the largest sprocket is the lowest gear. Going from a small rear sprocket to a larger one slows you down, but makes it easier to pedal.

On the rear derailleur, you will notice two wheel-like devices below the main body of the derailleur. The top one, nearest the derailleur, is the "jockey" wheel. It jockeys the chain back and forth from one sprocket to another just as the front derailleur does on the front chainwheel. Look at it while shifting the rear control lever to see how it works. The second, or lower wheel on the derailleur, is the "tension" wheel. Its job is to take up any slack in the chain and generally keep the chain under tension.

Reviewing these practice sessions at home helps alleviate any problem you may have encountered when shifting gears during your ride. You'll find out that it's not quite so easy to look down at the rear gears. Every time you try, you may find that you almost fall off your bicycle. Practicing at home where you can see the gears at work is one way to satisfy your curiosity.

Eventually, you will ride well enough to be able to look down at the rear gears without any trouble. However, you may also find out that by then you have learned enough about the gears that you don't have to look at them.

Hazards of the Road

Every venture out on the road requires the utmost in safety precautions. These precautions require being alert for road hazards and anticipating any traffic problems that might occur on the road. If a problem can be anticipated and a course of action thought out ahead of time, there most likely won't be any problems on the road for you.

Move with the traffic — not against it — as far to the right-hand side of the road as possible. Remember, your bicycle is a vehicle which has all the rights, privileges and responsibilities that automobiles do.

PARKED CARS AND TRAFFIC

Sooner or later you'll come to a parked car and have to negotiate around it. The first thing you must establish is that the car is stationary. A good habit to practice is looking into the rear windows of parked cars as you approach them. If someone is seated in the driver's seat, proceed with caution. Many a cyclist has been hurt by a car door suddenly opening in front of him or her.

Learn to look back over your left shoulder to check for approaching traffic. This is especially important if you're riding between parked cars, and traffic is moving in your same direction.

Also learn to recognize the sound of approaching traffic, however, don't over-depend on it. Purchase and install a rear-view mirror on your handlebars until you become accustomed to looking over your shoulder. Use the traffic sound as a signal to look behind you or into your rear-view mirror.

Our ears aren't acute enough to tell us what's coming, how close it is and the rate it's approaching. There are too many automobiles making too many sounds. Their sounds tend to blend together. That's why it is good practice to be alert and avoid veering out to the left after a car has passed.

GOING THROUGH INTERSECTIONS

Learn to start "playing" the signals at intersections. If you see that you are going to reach the intersection when the light is red, then slow down. It's much simpler to regulate your speed than to stop and start.

When stopping at an intersection, pull over to the right curb, and stop eight to 10 feet from the intersection. This allows you enough room from cars making right turns. When the light

Slit type drains are particularly dangerous. Once you get caught in one, there is no way to steer out.

changes, let turning cars go first. <u>You're not in a race</u> and there usually aren't that many cars making a right turn.

If you are going to make a right turn, slow down. Intersections provide sharp turns, and you may not be able to negotiate them yet. If you try to make the turn too fast, you'll find yourself swinging out too wide onto the path of traffic.

Left turns can be more of a problem. Legally, you can pull into the left lane near the center line, signal and turn just like any other vehicle. However, the safest way is a two-step procedure. First, ride straight through the intersection, staying on the right side of the street next to the curb. As soon as you are through the intersection, pull up to the curb and stop. Then, back your bicycle around the corner, remount and move ahead when the light changes, I've pedalled quite a few hundred miles, and I still follow this procedure.

Unlike many cyclists who write about city traffic, I don't think that the city driver is my sworn enemy. There is a very small percentage of automobile drivers who act as though they would prefer to drive over you rather than around you. However, I've found that most motorists are courteous and accommodating. They don't want to be involved in an accident any more than you do.

<u>Quite often, drivers don't</u> know what to do when they meet a <u>cyclist. They're not sure just where you</u> intend to ride and <u>they're not quite sure who has the right-of-way. Be courteous</u> <u>and cautious</u>.

WATCH FOR DEBRIS

One of the benefits of cycling is the joy of sightseeing. However, <u>keep your eyes on the road ahead of you, and watch</u> <u>for hazardous debris.</u> As you gain more experience, you'll be able to do this with rapid glances, but first it will take all your attention.

Suppose you are riding along, and ahead of you the road is littered with broken glass. If you're sure there is no traffic coming up behind you, and if you have time to turn, you can ride out into the road and avoid the glass. Yet, if you hear an approaching car behind you there are only two alternatives: you can stop, or ride through and hope for the best. <u>Avoid</u>

As soon as the rider crosses the first set of tracks he'll steer to the left, and cross the second set at right angles.

brake-slamming panic stops, for they can skid you into the road or curb or tumble you onto the glass. The important thing is to remember not to drastically veer out into the road automatically.

Steer clear of chuckholes and ruts, but avoid the "panic whip" where your first reaction is to whip the handlebars violently. You either shoot out into the center of the road or upset your bicycle. If you cannot avoid them, grasp the handlebars firmly and stand up just a bit on one pedal. Coasting over these hazards will give you better control of the bicycle.

Be careful when crossing railroad tracks. Those tracks crossing the road at right angles usually mean only a few uncomfortable bumps to the rider. The ones you have to watch out for are those that cross the road at about a 45-degree angle. Your front wheel can get caught and you can get thrown. Try to turn into the track and go over it as close to right angles as possible. The same is true of any narrow ruts you may be forced to ride over.

Water flowing across the street should be negotiated as slowly as possible. Going slowly to keep from getting sprayed by the water from the bicycle wheel is the minor reason. More importantly, you have no way of knowing if the water has been running one minute or one hour. If it has been running one hour, it may have flushed the area clean of mud and dirt, but it could just as easily be dumping a steady stream of mud on the road.

If it has been raining just a few minutes, that's just long enough to turn the accumulated dirt to slippery mud but not long enough to wash it away. In areas where it rains frequently, the streets are generally clean, and all you have to contend with is the normal slickness caused by the rain. If you live in a place where it rarely rains, be very careful. The rain will make the accumulated oil and grease on the road especially treacherous.

On one of my first rides I was riding along when I suddenly realized that there were several lawn sprinklers turned on just ahead. They were spraying quite a bit of water directly in my path. My first reaction was to swing out. Fortunately, I didn't, for there was a car just behind me. So I ducked down and coasted through. A little water won't hurt you, but swinging out suddenly to the left just might.

The grating in the foreground shows how difficult it is to see this hazard while bicycling.

Watch out for grating over drains! Grating is mainly found at the entrance to the sewer lines at most intersections. Getting your wheel caught between the grating irons can throw you for a loop, and damage your front wheel.

Remember to look over your shoulder before attempting to negotiate around the grating. If traffic is flowing too close, then stop and walk your bike over the grating. This will save you a lot of pain and money.

Avoid travelling over gravel or dirt roads. However, if you can't avoid this hazard, the best way to get through is to gear down to about fifth or sixth gear. This gives you more control on the pedals. Then pedal slowly but steadily, without coasting. Don't "drive" too hard, but move slowly and steadily, and pray for pavement.

SAFETY RULES AND PROCEDURES

Your bicycle is considered a vehicle like any other automobile, truck or motorcycle on the road. You are responsible for your actions just like any other driver, and you must obey the traffic laws just as they do.

Ride on the right side of the road, and stay in your lane or bike path. Since your bicycle is a vehicle, you have the right to fully occupy the right lane. However, it's better practice to stick to the right side of the road.

It's a good idea to be unobtrusive and not to force yourself into a heavy traffic flow. Choose an alternate route which runs parallel to the busy street and that has less traffic. This way you can enjoy your ride without worrying about motorists coming up from behind you.

Obey all traffic signs and signals. Many cyclists feel that these signs and signals don't apply to them. Not obeying a sign or running a red light at an intersection puts you in a situation and a place the motorist doesn't expect you to be.

Always think ahead. Get into the habit of checking parked cars, driveways and alley entrances. Assume that the motorist cannot see you approaching. Remember, motorists in general are programmed to only check for approaching cars. Be especially cautious in residential districts. It's those people who back out of their driveways while not looking back who are often the most careless. Bike defensively.

INJURIES

Never make the mistake of trying to "ride out" an injury. A strained muscle or tendon isn't going to be helped by riding. This only aggravates the injury more. Get off your bicycle, and stay off until the injury is completely healed. Don't mistake a sprain for muscular soreness, and try to ride the injury out of discomfort.

Usually you can ignore such things as brush burns, provided they aren't in some place where riding will aggravate them. I had a real nasty brush burn on one knee, but I was lucky. I didn't miss any days riding. On the other hand, a friend of mine fell and hit his knee in almost exactly the same place. His knee didn't have a mark on it, only a slight swelling. Nonetheless, he injured some ligaments, and it was nearly three months before he could ride again.

Riding is not the way to make injuries heal. Consult your doctor or physician who is knowledgeable about cycling injuries.

I've tried to use the exerciser, or exercycle, as I call it. However, I've never had much success with it.

When you are on a bicycle, every downward stroke of the pedals makes the bicycle sway from side to side. This sway may be so slight for an experienced rider that he or she doesn't notice it.

The stationary exerciser doesn't have this subtle movement. I have always felt limited and constrained while riding an exerciser. After hundreds of miles on a bicycle, I've established a very definite rhythm and pattern while pedalling. The exerciser didn't have that pattern. In addition, I kept getting painful twinges in my knees.

COPING WITH DOGS

One of the main hazards you're going to meet on the streets is man's best friend, the dog. I have come to the conclusion that how you react when a dog chases you depends primarily on how you feel toward dogs. If you are afraid of dogs, your actions are likely to be defensive and bent toward fleeing. If you aren't afraid of dogs, you may try to calm the dog.

As soon as you see a loose dog near you, watch him closely. Many will simply ignore you. For some reason, larger dogs will often ignore you more than small ones. Whatever he does, make a quick decision whether or not you can outrun him. With larger dogs, you usually can't, unless a dog is an overweight St. Bernard. You may outrun him in the long run. However, unless he's a good distance away when he starts after you, he can usually catch up with you. That's your first choice – try to outrun him.

In my case, the very first time I had a dog chase me I was riding on a steep uphill climb doing about four miles an hour. There was just no way I was going to outrun him. He was one of the small yapping types and ill tempered to boot. He really looked like he intended to bite.

I stopped and picked up a handful of pebbles and threw a few at him. I threw them pretty hard, but I deliberately missed. I didn't want to hurt him. I just wanted him to know that I wasn't something that could be attacked at will. I got on my bicycle and threw a handful of pebbles gently in his direction. As he backed off I pedalled around the next curve and out of his territory.

I've tried other things. I've waited until the last moment and then reached back with one foot and banged a vicious looking German police dog on the nose with my foot. I've yelled at some dogs, swung my hat at others.

Some people suggest carrying noisemakers or squirt guns with some unpleasant liquid in them. There's a little bottle of compressed air for sale at some bicycle shops. It has a small horn attached to it and it can make a terrible noise.

I'm against these things for several reasons. I may ride for two weeks without being chased by a single dog. I'm not going to lug something around for two weeks just to use it for a few seconds. Another problem with those horns and squirt guns is that you have to get them out of your pocket, grasp the trigger, aim and then use them. By that time the dog has already bitten you a couple of times. Nevertheless, I'm against squirt guns with various liquids in them, because I don't want to take a chance on injuring the dog. While I'm not a fanatic about dogs, I do like them. I see no reason to hurt or harm one if there is any other possible way of resolving the situation.

Perhaps the most practical advice is to act here as you would act elsewhere with a dog. If you are afraid of dogs, then do the following when one chases you. Stop and get off your bicycle. Keep it between you and the dog. Wait awhile. Many dogs will lose interest and wander away. If the dog does not, start walking your bicycle down the street. Most dogs have their territorial limits. Once you cross the border, they lose interest.

I use a somewhat different system. But I'm not afraid of dogs. And they seem to know it.

First, I stop and get off my bicycle. If there is any chance of making friends with the dog, I do so. I may stay and play with him until he wanders off. But if I see he just isn't going to be friendly, I usually head straight for him. No pauses, no uncertainty, no hesitation. This will usually unnerve him enough that he will turn and go away. I will go after him for a bit. But I never try to corner him. If he insists on standing his ground, he gets a sharp bang on the nose. (I don't like dogs enough to let one bite me.) But in all of this, I'm not afraid of the dog and I never show hesitation.

I have several friends who are meter readers, and they tell me that this immediate frontal approach usually works for them, but mainly with larger dogs. The smaller yapping types keep bouncing around and barking.

There is one other thing to remember. A dog in a yard is defending his own territory. He will fight harder and faster than one in the open.

Most dogs are reasonably good natured and very few are vicious. And as a result of that attitude, I've found that I get into a lot less trouble with dogs than people who hate and/or fear them.

Getting in Shape

Any ride is long if you think it is. When I was just beginning to ride, I had a 2.1-mile loop I used to ride. On my third day of riding in the street, I made four complete trips around the loop. I had ridden 8.4 miles! I was shaking with exhaustion, but I can still remember how proud I was.

Rides of 15 to 25 miles are considered by most cyclists as short rides. A medium ride would be 25 to 40 miles and anything from 40 to 70 miles is considered a long ride. There are Century rides, of course, where the rider goes 100 miles in one day. However, these are special events and few racing cyclists will travel that far on a normal day's ride.

Just riding around your neighborhood can be fun. During weekdays, when your time is limited, it is probably the only practical place to ride. But as your strength and abilities increase, you will soon find yourself growing restless. You start to feel that there is a whole world out there and you aren't getting to see any of it. You start thinking about the longer ride.

So what is a longer ride for the beginning cyclist? Your first "long" rides should be no more than 20 to 30 miles. As you ride greater and greater distances, different things happen to your body. It is important to get used to these things a few at a time.

LONG-DISTANCE PREPARATION

The best way to prepare for truly longer rides is to do it

gradually. Get used to the shorter rides you cycle during the week. Work your way up to longer distances a little at a time. Don't attempt successive rides of 25, 35 and 45 miles. Take three or four 25- to 30-mile rides before going on to a 35-mile ride. It is only after you have mastered one distance that you should go on to a longer ride.

The way to extend your range is simple: you ride and ride often. By the end of the first summer, you can be doing rides of 50 miles a day or longer. Building your endurance is like building a stone wall. A stone wall is not built out of one single piece, but out of hundreds of bricks. Endurance is built the same way, a piece at a time. Every tireless rider you see has scores of rides behind him where he has built up his endurance bit by bit, block by block. You can build yours the same way.

ADAPTING TO STRESS

Endurance doesn't have to be built up only on weekends. You can do it during the week. Select a route near your home—preferably one with as few stops and traffic signals as possible. Take the same route over and over, and time yourself every day. Timing yourself while trying to go increasingly faster doesn't mean you are trying to turn yourself into a racing cyclist. It simply means that you are keeping a record of your early progress. Every day you'll have to work a little harder, placing a bit more stress on your body. You begin to learn what it can do and what it cannot do. You can feel yourself growing stronger.

During the first weeks of riding, you will be amazed at how much your times improve. I discovered a 6.6-mile loop route near my home. Included in the route was a three-quarter-mile climb. The first time I took this trip, it took me 64 minutes, and I later decreased my time to 26 minutes. You can do the same with the routes you choose.

Hard riding, short rides are not the same as long rides. But they are the building blocks upon which you can begin to build skills for those longer rides.

BURNING UP CALORIES

Cycling is strenuous exercise and consumes large amounts of calories. An easy-going cyclist can use 200-300 calories an hour.

A racing cyclist may use as much as 600 calories an hour. Most of us are not likely to get up to the 600 calorie an hour level, however, we still use up more calories than we are used to using. We obtain energy, or calories, by eating and we expend energy when we work.

In order to derive the most enjoyment from riding, you'll have to learn to pace yourself in such a way that you do not ask your body to supply energy at a rate which is greater than it can handle. I am not saying that you have to learn how to keep from getting tired. That's impossible. What I am saying is that you must learn to judge when you're beginning to overexert yourself so that you can slow down to avoid such a problem. It may seem as though I am stating the obvious, but I have found this to be one of the most difficult things of all to learn. Everyone understands what you mean when you talk about pacing yourself. Nonetheless, knowing what something means and knowing how to apply it are two different things.

The amount of energy you have available on any given day is determined primarily by how well you rested, how wisely you ate, your age, your health, your physical condition and your body build. The efficiency of your cycling, the kind of bicycle you have, the terrain you are going to ride over do not have anything to do with the amount of energy stored. These factors only determine how fast and how far you can ride with the energy you have available.

As you can see, the problem of pacing yourself is not as simple as it appears to be at first. There are complicating factors. As the days go by, you grow stronger and your endurance increases. With proper pacing, you ride more efficiently and a lot further on the same amount of energy.

JUDGING YOUR STRENGTH

So what good is it to know how much energy you have available on a given day? Energy pacing permits you to plan your riding. It enables you to determine beforehand whether or not you have the strength to complete a certain ride. Most of us have never engaged in activities where we actually had to sit down and estimate whether or not we had enough energy to perform a certain task.

At first, you learn the pacing process backwards. You take a ride first and then determine how you feel afterward. After a few weeks of making this conscious effort, you begin to have a good idea of how much you can *actually* do, and not how much you *think* you can do. In addition, you will be able to judge your strength at any point before, during or after a ride.

One of the problems in learning how to pace is that few people normally engage in activities so demanding as cycling. While on vacation you may decide that 250 miles is all you can drive in one day. Then you find that you want to go on for another 50 or 75 miles. You may be tired, but you can still find the strength to drive that extra distance. You cannot do that when cycling. If your limit for one day is 40 miles, believe me, it is 40 miles.

ENERGY CONSUMPTION

You should divide your rides into two groups: group one consists of rides of up to 25 miles; group two consists of rides of 25 miles or longer. If you're in good shape and have taken rides between 15 and 20 miles, you don't have to make any real eating plans for rides up to 25 miles. About all you need to take along with you is a bottle of water. If you have eaten a decent meal before you begin, you already have enough energy to sustain you for the entire ride.

Rides of 25 miles or longer are another matter. On a normal day, Americans generally eat enough to have sufficient energy to do whatever tasks they have at hand. Even if they miss a meal, they can usually go on for the rest of the day without too much trouble. This system doesn't work out too well for the cyclist taking longer rides. A cyclist can easily use up all the energy consumed at breakfast well before the next normal mealtime.

Take along some high energy food snacks for your longer rides. Some riders eat a high energy fruit bar every 30 minutes or every hour. Others will stop at preplanned points and have a snack. How much and how often you eat is something you should experiment with. Accept the fact that you have to eat on longer rides whether you want to or not.

Get used to the idea of eating regularly *on schedule* and not just when you get hungry. It takes a while for the body to turn food into energy. Remember, it's hard to move a bicycle when your energy has been depleted.

PACING YOURSELF

Knowing your physical limitations is one of the most important aspects of cycling. In order to enjoy a simple ride through the countryside or surpass the grueling test of a Century ride, you'll have to learn how to pace yourself in such a way that permits your body to efficiently expend energy during a long-distance ride. The following examples illustrate how proper pacing can help.

● Don't waste energy at the beginning of a ride. Late in my first summer of cycling I reached the point of riding 45 to 60 miles every Saturday. On one particular Saturday I had selected a circular 55-mile ride over flat countryside.

The day was perfect. The weather was clear and crisp, and there was a mild tailwind. The road was as flat and smooth as a billiard table and had a superb three-foot-wide bike trail marked off on the roadside. I felt great, bubbling over with energy. I decided to go all out.

For more than an hour I went down on the lower handlebars and really blasted away. I covered over 20 miles. Not fast for a racing cyclist, but very fast for me. Finally, I stopped for a rest. I still felt good, but the effervescent feeling was gone.

The next 25 miles were good miles and I felt reasonably strong. Then, all of a sudden I ran out of energy. That's when I realized my mistake. The extra energy I wasted while going too fast on those first 20 miles was energy I needed but didn't have. I managed to struggle through those last 12 miles.

I didn't underpace myself at the beginning of the long ride. If I would have paced myself wisely, I could have had enough energy when I needed it.

● Know how much energy you have available before reaching your limit. I ran into a different kind of pacing problem during my second summer of riding. I had planned a ride of about 60 miles: the first 20 miles would cover flat ground, the next 10 would be up and down a very steep road, then 30 miles back home.

I got to the bottom of the steep road in good shape and could handle most of the grades. However, some of the switchbacks were extremely steep. The steep grades took every ounce of strength I had, and I usually had to stop and rest as soon as I finished climbing.

After about the third such switchback, I stopped to think about it. I still had four more uphill miles to go, five miles downhill, then 30 miles home. I stopped to estimate how much energy I had left. I soon realized I didn't have enough energy to make the trip if I rode up that steep road. I decided to walk my bicycle up the steeper switchbacks. (Walking my bicycle is something I hate to do. It is like admitting defeat.) I did it because I knew that one cannot move a bicycle forward on will power and ego alone: one needs energy. If I had ridden all the way up that hill, I would have never made it home.

● Whenever stopping to rest, monitor your immediate physical condition from two viewpoints: determine how tired you are in a superficial sense, and how tired you are in an overall sense.

Here is what I mean by getting tired in a superficial sense. We all have times when we start gasping for breath, and we feel we can't make another turn of the pedals. So we stop to take a breather. In two or three minutes we are ready to go again.

Nonetheless, we are also getting tired in an overall sense. No matter how fresh we feel after that short break, we are no longer as fresh as when we started. How fast we are tiring in an overall sense is an important guide to knowing if we are pushing ourselves too hard. This third pacing problem is one of the most common among beginning riders. It usually occurs when beginners try to keep up with riders far more experienced than they are.

Remember the three basics of long-distance pacing. Don't waste energy at the beginning of a ride that you may need at the end. Get to know how much energy you have available before you use it all up, and know when you are asking too much, too fast of your body.

There is one other point to remember when pacing yourself: establish a steady cadence. You ride most efficiently when you

Serious Cycling for the Beginner

can maintain the same number of pedal revolutions per minute from the beginning of a ride to the end. This can cause problems on longer rides. You may start out the day at 65 rpm in a 72-inch gear and find pedalling easy. Thirty-five miles later, you may find it almost impossible. The answer, of course, is to gear down the number of gears you need to enable you to maintain your cadence. There is nothing wrong in starting a ride in a 72-inch gear and ending up in a 49-inch gear. Remember to use a gear *that makes pedalling easy*. One common error occurs when the cyclist insists on believing that he or she is not really cycling unless the bicycle is in a gear which makes it hard to move the pedals. Forget that. Use a gear that makes riding easy. Know your limits and maintain the proper cadence.

6
Uphill Riding and Gears

You are your bicycle's engine. Your body supplies the energy to move you forward. As long as you are moving forward at a moderate speed on a lightly loaded bicycle over level ground, you generally have no problems. Certain demands for energy output are being made on your body. If your body can meet these requirements, there's no overriding need for a gearing system.

What happens if you load up your bicycle with extra weight or have to ride your bike uphill? Suddenly, the demands for energy output become greater. When they become so great that your body cannot meet them, you become tired and are forced to stop. Like an engine, your body becomes overheated and stalls.

The gearing system of a 10-speed bicycle permits you to adjust the rate of demands for energy output to a level your body can handle. For instance, you are riding along at a moderate speed over level ground and the gears are set in one of the middle gears so that you're pedalling at a good and untiring rate. You soon arrive at the foot of a steep hill. Until now your body supplied enough energy to move you and the bicycle forward. Now, your body is asked to provide enough energy to push you and the bicycle 500 feet up a steep grade. You have several alternatives:

- You can turn around and go back. If you don't gear down, this may be the wisest choice.

- You can stay in the same gear and keep pedalling at the same rate as before. Nevertheless, pedalling has become so difficult that you have to strain with every downward stroke of the pedals. If the hill is too steep, you may not be able to pedal at all. In any case, you'll become exhausted very quickly and have to rest.

• You can shift down to a lower gear, which allows you to pedal as fast as before, but with the bicycle wheels turning at a slower rate. The total demands for energy being made on your body have not been reduced, but they have been spread out over a longer period of time.

RIDING GRADUAL RISES

This gradual uphill grade has a tendency to sneak up on you. Your car has been rolling up and down these rises for years with no effort, and you have come to ignore them. However, you certainly realize these gradual rises are there the first time you try to cycle over them.

Get into the habit of occasionally glancing at least a block ahead and recognizing gradual rises. Learn to stop the foot of the rise: the point where the road begins to go uphill. Then, when you're about 50 to 75 feet away, start shifting down a gear or two. This is more distance than you may need.

Shifting gears while riding uphill is something to be avoided whenever possible. The gears will shift reluctantly with a loud jangling sound, placing too much strain on the derailleur and the whole gear system. In addition, the chain can jam or slip off the front chainwheel or rear sprockets. Remember, the less tension

You should be able to handle this grade on your first rides.

You may have to down shift on these gradual rises to maintain a constant cadence.

there is on the chain, the easier it is to shift gears. For this reason it's best to shift while going downhill or riding on a level surface.

Gradual rises provide a good opportunity for practicing to gear down. The object here is to become acquainted with shifting — not to see how fast you can shift.

Don't worry about shifting down too low. If pedalling is still difficult, shift down again. However, if you feel that you've shifted down too low and that pedalling is too easy, don't shift back. Go to the top of the grade in the same gear. I've shifted up one gear only to find that I chose the right gear in the first place.

Struggling up a slight grade can be discouraging if you don't know the grade's difficulty ahead of time. However, within a couple of weeks, you should be negotiating those same long, gradual rises more easily. What's more, you'll be able to take most of them in fifth or sixth gear where you once struggled up in second or third gear.

RIDING SHORT GRADES

Small grades or hills are those in a range of 10 to 30 feet high and aren't more than 100 yards long. The successful small hill climb for the beginner starts a hundred feet or so before reaching the bottom of the hill. The following page tells how this method is accomplished.

- Develop a good speed while on level ground, and coast for approximately a second. Then begin to pedal slow enough to keep the rear wheel from engaging with the gears. Now downshift. The gears should shift easily. Finally, increase your pedalling rate, allowing the rear wheel to engage again.
- Try to complete the shift about 10 feet from the foot of the hill. Then settle down to a steady pace before reaching the bottom of the hill. If the hill is a fairly steep grade, use a 40-inch gear or lower (depending on the steepness and length of the grade). Choosing a gear higher than that could give you trouble.
- Go down to the lower handlebars as you begin the hill. When pedalling, try to push forward a bit when your foot is at 12 o'clock and then push down. Remember to ride on the balls of your feet, pull against the handlebars if you need to, and maintain a slow, steady pace until you reach the top.
- When you start down the other side, shift into high gear. Then pedal downhill until the wheels are turning so fast that you can't engage them. Keep your downhill speed reasonable. (If you get beyond a certain speed, the smallest rock or bump becomes most hazardous.)

THE UPHILL CHALLENGE

For more demanding climbs like long and continuous uphill roads, take rest stops whenever pedalling becomes too cumbersome, or you'll become overtaxed. Some uphill roads can rise as much as a thousand feet over a distance of several miles, causing many beginning cyclists to initially give up the challenge.

It is important to assess your immediate physical condition on these long uphill grades. (Same holds true for short rises.) Are you fresh enough to accept the challenge or do you feel tired? Are you breathing lightly or panting heavily? Do your legs feel strong, or do they feel heavy and tired? Even the strongest rider can be defeated by a hill if he's too tired at the start.

Riding up a long grade or mountain road may initially call for a number of stops along the way. It's good practice to take these rest stops and make note of their locations. This will enable you to gauge your progress.

On long uphill climbs, it's essential for the beginning cyclist to go as slow as possible.

Before reaching the foot of this long uphill climb, shift your bicycle into low gear, and maintain a slow, steady pace until you reached the top or you're forced to stop. In this low gear pedalling will be easy, and the temptation of pedalling harder or shifting to a higher gear will become greater. It's good practice to resist this temptation and regulate your energy output.

RIDING DOWNHILL

There is one final point which needs mentioning about uphill riding. What goes up must come down. A real downhill run can be tremendously exhilarating. It can also be dangerous if you aren't careful.

Watch out for sand and dirt piled up at curves. Running into them can flip you over the front wheel. If they are deep, they can slide the wheels out from beneath you. Don't let the bicycle run away from you. Once you get beyond a certain speed, things seem to change. The smallest bumps can nearly unseat you, for the bicycle is less stable.

Approach curves carefully whenever going downhill. I got

carried away once and took a curve too fast. The centrifugal force made me feel as if a giant hand was trying to push me off the road as I went around the curve. Try to keep the pedal on the inside of a turn at the 12 o'clock position. Even when your bicycle is level the pedal is only a few inches from the ground. When you lean into a sharp turn, that pedal can get very close to the ground. Normally, you shouldn't ride so close to the curb that the right pedal will hit it.

Try to do most of your braking before you hit a curve, and remember to use both brakes at the same time. Never slam on the brakes. Hold your speed down by gradually squeezing the brakes, releasing them and squeezing them again.

One of the trickiest things to watch for is a crosswind. You can be going downhill where there is no breeze at all, round a curve and nearly get knocked down by a vicious crosswind. Your chances of not falling are best if you keep your speed down and stay alert.

If you started up a hill similar to this one, you should have completed changing gears at the point of the nearest car in the foreground.

Control Levers

Chainwheel

Crank

Front Derailleur

Chain Guide

Control Cable

Rear Sprocket
Cluster

Jockey Roller

Tension Roller

Rear
Derailleur

Direction of
Chain Movement

POWER TRAIN

GEARING SYSTEM

The gearing system on a 10-speed is not a magic device which eliminates effort. It merely regulates the rate at which you have to produce energy. A certain amount of energy is needed to raise an object 500 feet no matter how it's done. In high gear you were asked to produce a substantial amount of energy in a short time. The low gear allows you to produce the same amount of energy over a longer period of time at a rate you can handle.

First gear is the same as in your car. It is the lowest gear: the one used for difficult or uphill low-speed riding. Tenth gear is high gear for downhill high-speed riding. Fourth, fifth and sixth gears are your middle gears used for moderate bicycling through residential streets.

GEAR RANGES

On a 10-speed bicycle, you always have two front chainwheels. These two chainwheels have considerably more teeth than the rear sprockets. On both front and rear, the sprockets closest to the bicycle body are the low gears. The ones farthest away are the high gears. The larger of the two front chainwheels is the higher speed. On most bicycles, the larger chainwheel has 48, 50 or 52 teeth. The more teeth there are on the larger chainwheel, the higher the gear for faster speeds.

The narrower the difference between the two front chainwheels, the narrower the range of gears one through 10. If your bicycle has a large chainwheel with 52 teeth and a small one with 48 teeth, then it's a bicycle designed for either a very experienced rider or for use on fairly level ground. A bicycle with a large chainwheel of 52 teeth and a small one with 42 to 46 teeth is designed for the average rider and should be able to negotiate varied types of terrain.

A bicycle with a large chainwheel of 52 teeth and a small one of 36 to 42 teeth is designed for use by a beginning rider or for use on hilly terrain. The first bicycle I owned had front chainwheels with 52 and 36 teeth. It was perfectly designed for a middle-aged inexperienced rider such as myself.

However, the greater the difference between the two front chainwheels, the more difficult it is for the derailleur to move the chain from one sprocket to the other, forcing a greater strain on the chain and front derailleur. This can often add up to more maintenance problems. But if you need a wide range, get it. There is no point in having a maintenance-free bicycle you can't ride.

The general range of the number of teeth on the smaller chainwheel is wider and can range from a low of about 36 teeth to a high of about 48 teeth.

On both front and rear, the chainwheel or sprockets closest to the bicycle frame are the low gears. Those rear sprockets or front chainwheel farthest away are the high gears.

The number of teeth on rear sprockets generally range from 14 to 34 teeth. Some bicycles go lower than 14 teeth, but I've never heard of a bicycle's rear sprocket with more than 34 teeth, although I suppose some do exist.

A chain going around a 14-tooth sprocket places you in a high gear, which is meant for high-speed use. Those sprockets with a range of 18-22 teeth are used for average cycling. Sprockets having between 24 and 28 teeth are for uphill riding. The 34-tooth sprocket is for very steep uphill riding.

REAR SPROCKET COMBINATIONS

There are many combinations available for the five-sprocket rear wheel. You can get a set with 14, 15, 16, 17 and 18 teeth, or one with 15, 19, 20, 25, 26 teeth, or any combination that you want. The thing you must do, of course, is to consider very carefully what size sprockets are on the chainwheel and what kind of riding you have in mind.

For example, a set of rear sprockets with 14, 16, 18, 20 and 22 teeth provides a narrow range and is meant for the very experienced rider or for use on level ground only. A range of 14 to 26 teeth is for the intermediate rider. Many bicycles have rear wheel sprocket clusters ranging from 14 to 26 or 28 teeth. This provides a good range for most cyclists. However, if you are a beginner or plan a lot of uphill riding, a range of 14 to 31 or even 34 teeth would be appropriate.

In sum, front chainwheels have teeth ranging in number from 36 to 52. The rear sprockets range from 14 to 34. The narrower the range, the less difference between low gear and high gear.

You now begin to realize that you have two sets of sprockets which complement each other.

GEAR RATIOS

In order to have some way of putting things in order, a system is used to determine gear ratio of any combination of front chainwheel and rear sprockets. Let's say that the chain on our imaginary bicycle is on the smallest rear sprocket which has 14 teeth and on the largest front chainwheel with 52 teeth. That would be your highest or 10th gear. What is the gear ratio of this combination?

We use the following formula:

$$\frac{\text{Teeth On Chainwheel}}{\text{Teeth On Rear Sprocket}} \times 27 = \text{Gear Ratio}$$

Or, in our example, $52/14 \times 27 = 100.3$.

The gear ratio at that setting is 100.3, and the bicycle is said to be in a 100-inch gear.

Let's say that you have set the chain around the 14-tooth sprocket and the smaller chainwheel, which has 36 teeth. What gear are you in?

Answer: $36/14 \times 27 = 69.4$ or a 69-inch gear.

By using this formula you can make some sense out of the various settings. The chart on the following page will aid you in figuring out gears (or gear ratios).

A 35-inch gear is about as low as most average bicycles go. You can certainly get one with a lower gear, but you'll usually have to ask for it. The 35- to 42-inch gear range is generally used for heavy loads on level ground or steep uphill climbing. To use such a low gear on level ground without a heavy load is as tiring as using too high a gear.

A 42-inch gear to a 60-inch gear is used on mild grades, with mild loads or pedalling into a heavy wind.

A 60-inch gear to about a 75-inch gear is used for level ground cruising. When I have a long steady ride ahead on level ground I use a 72-inch gear.

An 80-inch gear to about a 105-inch gear is for high speed

TEETH ON REAR SPROCKETS

	36	37	38	39	40	41	42	43	44
14	69.4	71.4	73.3	75.2	77.1	79.1	81.0	82.9	84.9
15	64.8	66.6	68.4	70.2	72.0	73.8	75.6	77.4	79.2
16	60.8	62.4	64.1	65.8	67.5	69.2	70.9	72.6	74.3
17	57.2	58.8	60.4	61.9	63.5	65.1	66.7	68.3	69.9
18	54.0	55.5	57.0	58.5	60.0	61.5	63.0	64.5	66.0
19	51.2	52.6	54.0	55.4	54.8	58.3	59.7	61.1	62.5
20	48.6	50.0	51.3	52.7	54.0	55.4	56.7	58.1	59.4
21	46.3	47.6	48.9	50.1	51.4	52.7	54.0	55.3	56.6
22	44.2	45.4	46.6	47.9	49.1	50.3	51.5	52.8	54.0
23	42.3	43.4	44.6	45.8	47.0	48.1	49.3	50.5	51.7
24	40.5	41.6	42.8	43.9	45.0	46.1	47.3	48.4	49.5
25	38.9	40.0	41.0	42.1	43.2	44.3	45.4	46.4	47.5
26	37.4	38.4	39.5	40.5	41.5	42.6	43.6	44.7	45.7
27	36	37	38.0	39.0	40.0	41.0	42.0	43.0	44.0
28	34.7	35.7	36.6	37.6	38.6	39.5	40.5	41.5	42.4
29	33.5	34.5	35.4	36.3	37.2	38.2	39.1	40.0	41.0
30	32.4	33.3	34.2	35.1	36.0	36.9	37.8	38.7	39.6
31	31.4	32.2	33.1	34.0	34.8	35.7	36.6	37.5	38.3
32	30.4	31.2	32.1	32.9	33.8	34.6	35.4	37.1	37.1
33	29.5	30.3	31.1	31.9	32.7	33.6	34.4	35.2	36.0
34	28.6	29.4	30.2	31.0	31.8	32.6	33.4	34.2	34.9

GEAR

CHAINWHEELS (SPROCKETS)

45	46	47	48	49	50	51	52	53	54
86.8	88.7	90.6	92.6	94.5	96.4	98.4	100.3	102.2	104.1
81.0	82.8	84.6	86.4	88.2	90.0	91.8	93.6	95.4	97.2
75.9	77.6	79.3	81.0	82.7	84.4	86.1	87.8	89.4	91.1
71.5	73.1	74.6	76.2	77.8	79.4	81.0	82.6	89.2	85.8
67.5	69.0	70.5	72.0	73.5	75.0	76.5	78.0	79.5	81.0
64.0	65.4	66.8	68.2	69.6	71.1	72.5	73.9	75.3	76.7
60.8	62.1	63.5	64.8	66.2	67.5	68.9	70.2	71.6	72.9
57.9	59.1	60.4	61.7	63.0	64.3	65.6	66.9	68.1	69.4
55.2	56.5	57.7	58.9	60.1	61.4	62.6	63.8	65.0	66.3
52.8	54.0	55.2	56.4	57.5	58.7	59.9	61.0	62.2	63.4
50.6	51.7	52.9	54.0	55.1	56.3	57.4	58.5	59.6	60.8
48.6	49.7	50.8	51.8	52.9	54.0	55.1	56.2	57.2	58.3
46.7	47.8	48.8	49.8	50.9	51.9	53.0	54.0	55.0	56.1
45.0	46.0	47.0	48.0	49.0	50.0	51.0	52.0	53.0	54.0
43.4	44.4	45.3	46.3	47.3	48.2	49.2	50.1	51.1	52.1
41.9	42.8	43.8	44.7	45.6	46.6	47.5	48.4	49.3	50.3
40.5	41.4	42.3	43.2	44.1	45.0	45.9	46.8	47.7	48.6
39.2	40.1	41.0	41.8	42.7	43.6	44.4	45.3	46.2	47.0
38.0	38.8	39.7	40.5	51.3	42.2	43.0	43.9	44.7	45.6
36.8	37.6	38.5	39.3	40.1	40.9	41.7	42.5	43.4	44.2
35.7	36.5	37.3	38.1	38.9	39.7	40.5	41.3	42.1	42.9

RATIOS

riding, downhill or with a good wind at your back.

GEAR ARRANGEMENT

Now let's start filling things in by determining if you have a 10-speed bicycle or an eight- or nine-speed one.

On my first 10-speed, the chainwheel had sprockets of 52 and 36 teeth. On the rear, it had sprockets with 14, 17, 21, 24 and 28 teeth. The chart already mentioned has most of these combinations already worked out for you. Use it to figure out what your own gear ratios are. Or use the aforementioned formula to find your gears.

36-Tooth Front Gear	52-Tooth Front Gear
14 - 36 = 69.4 gear	14 - 52 = 100.3 gear
17 - 36 = 57.2	17 - 52 = 82.6
21 - 36 = 46.2	21 - 52 = 66.9
24 - 36 = 40.5	24 - 52 = 58.5
28 - 36 = 34.7	28 - 52 = 50.1

Now let's put those gear ratios into numerical order starting from the lowest gear: first gear − 34.7, second gear − 40.5, third gear − 46.2, fourth gear − 50.1, fifth gear − 57.2, sixth gear − 58.5, seventh gear − 66.9, eighth gear − 69.4, ninth gear − 82.6, tenth gear − 100.3.

Look at the fifth and sixth gears and at the seventh and eighth gears. They are almost the same. In fifth gear the chain was on the 17-36 rear sprocket/chainwheel combination. In the sixth gear the chain was on the 24-52 set. Again, the gear ratio is almost the same. Now you can see that it's possible to have a bicycle with 10 gear changes and only eight gears.

This arrangement has other faults. Look at the jump between fourth and fifth gears and sixth and seventh gears. That's quite an increase. If I wanted to go slightly up or down in those ranges, I couldn't do it. In addition, there's quite a jump in the last two gears. The increase in the high gears is always greater than the lower ones but an increase of 30.9 in only two gear changes is quite large.

When I walked into the bicycle shop to purchase a bicycle, I knew absolutely nothing about bicycles or gears. I was 45 years old and 15 pounds overweight.

The salesman took one look at me and knew that I needed a bicycle with a low gear. The 36-tooth chainwheel combined with the 28-tooth rear sprocket gave me a low gear of 34.7. If I hadn't had that low gear in the beginning, I might well have become discouraged every time I came to a rise or hill.

The fact that some gears overlapped and some were far apart didn't hurt me that much. Those first weeks when you are learning to ride, you just aren't sophisticated enough in gear use to be even aware of the problem.

The big jump to ninth and tenth gears wasn't much of a bother those first weeks. I wasn't experienced or strong enough to use the high gears. As a matter of fact, I rode in low gears the first month. I would go up the gentlest of rises in first or second gear. Today I really don't notice the same rises as I go over them in seventh or eighth gear. If there are any generalizations that are true of beginners, it's that they use low gear too much, and they equate improvement with going into higher gears over the same course. Eventually, the beginner realizes the futility of this and uses a reasonable gear for the particular terrain.

Now let's take a look at the second bicycle I owned. The chainwheels have 54 and 48 teeth. The rear sprockets have 14, 18, 22, 27 and 34.

48-Tooth Chainwheel	54-Tooth Chainwheel
14 - 92.6	14 - 104.1
18 - 72.0	18 - 81.0
22 - 58.9	22 - 66.3
27 - 48.0	27 - 54.0
34 - 38.1	34 - 42.9

Now we can arrange them in order: first gear — 38.1, second gear — 42.9, third gear — 48.0, fourth gear — 54.0, fifth gear — 58.9, sixth gear — 66.3, seventh gear — 72.0, eighth gear — 81.0, ninth gear — 92.6, tenth gear — 104.1.

The difference between gears is fairly even, and there are no blank spots or big jumps from one gear to the next.

In addition, there is a wide range. The 54-tooth front

chainwheel, when combined with the 14-tooth rear sprocket provides a 104-inch top gear. The 48-tooth front chainwheel combined with the 34-tooth rear sprocket gives me a good low gear of 38.

ALTERNATING FRONT SPROCKETS

There is one more important point you should know. When changing from one gear to the next, you *don't* leave the chain on just one of the front sprockets for the first five gears and then move it to the other sprocket for the next five. The bicycle chain has to alternate back and forth on the front sprockets as well as on the rear ones.

The following combinations of front and rear sprockets produced a certain gear ratio. Notice that the chain has to go back and forth from the 48- to 54-tooth front sprockets.

Gear Combinations		Gear Ratio Produced
Rear	Front	
34	48	38.1
34	54	42.9
27	48	48.0
27	54	54.0
22	48	58.9
22	54	66.3
18	48	72.0
18	54	81.6
14	48	92.6
14	54	104.1

Alternating between both front sprockets is a common rule when changing gears from one through 10. It is important to remember this gear changing technique. Otherwise you'll be skipping gears rather than changing them in a consistantly flowing manner.

However, there are exceptions to this rule. For example, there may come a time when you purchase a bicycle which has two front sprockets with 52 and 36 teeth. This could cause some problem if you are not acquainted with the proper method of changing 52- and 36-tooth front sprockets. The gear settings for this unusual combination are on the following page.

Gear Combinations		Gear Ratio Produced
Rear	Front	
28	36	34.7
24	36	40.5
21	36	46.2
28	52	50.1
17	36	57.2
24	52	58.5
21	52	66.9
14	36	69.4
17	52	82.6
14	52	100.3

Due to the wide difference in the number of teeth between the two front chainwheels, the lower three gears (34.7, 40.5 and 46.2) are all achieved using the smaller of the front chainwheels. Four of the five highest gears are achieved using the 52-tooth front chainwheel (58.5, 66.9, 82.6 and 100.3).

If possible, get a 48- and 54-tooth chainwheel combination or one that creates a similar shifting pattern. Less orderly patterns are almost impossible to remember while you are riding. Incidentally, you can get just about any combination of sprockets you want for the bicycle you already have. You don't have to purchase a new bicycle in order to get new gears.

POINTS TO REMEMBER

● If you have a set of gears on your bicycle that has a narrow range and you want to replace them with gears having a wide range, you may have to get a new rear derailleur. One function of the rear derailleur is to move the chain from one sprocket to another. It must also take up the slack in the bicycle chain by keeping it under tension. If you make a drastic change in gears, the derailleur you have now may not have a wide enough range to handle the gear change. Some derailleurs do, but they are generally the more expensive ones meant for touring bicycles, and the chances are your present bicycle didn't come equipped with one.

● Don't become too preoccupied with getting real low gears.

One of the things new riders often want, once they understand the gears, is a set that go so low they can ride up the side of a building: something as low as 33-inch or 31-inch gear. If you are going to do a lot of cross-country touring, you may really need it. However, your first 500 miles you should be sticking close to home where you don't need such low gears as a 33 or a 31.

As you learn to use the gears, you will find yourself using the low gears less. On your first week or two you may go on a hilly ride where you spend the whole trip in the lower three or four gears. Six weeks later you will be sailing through the same trip in fourth through seventh or eighth gear.

● Take your dealer's advice on what kind of gears are being sold in your area. He's already sold many sets, and he knows how to take your age, physical condition and the local terrain into proper consideration.

The Last of the First 500 Miles

If you look at the feet of other cyclists as they go by, you'll notice that all of those who seem to be the most proficient have one thing in common. They have small metal cages around their feet and their feet are strapped to the pedals.

TOE STRAPS AND TOE CLIPS

Any cyclist who plans to ride for any distance should consider using toe straps and toe clips. The use of these two items will increase your cycling efficiency 30 to 40 per cent.

So how do they work? Let's look at the way you are pedalling now. Normally, most of us push down on one pedal from about the 2 o'clock position to the 6 o'clock position. After you get past that point, there isn't much you can do except let your foot sit on the pedal and be pushed upwards toward the 12 o'clock position by the downstroke of the other foot.

When your feet are strapped to the pedals, you can do all of the things described above. Furthermore, when your foot reaches the 6 o'clock position, you can pull *up* with that foot from the 6 o'clock position, to the 10 o'clock position. Strapping your feet to the pedal accomplishes the following:

● It removes the weight of the foot going up and makes pressing down easier.

● By pulling up with one foot, it reduces the work load for the foot pushing down.

- Instead of making one set of muscles do all the work while the other set gets a free ride, it makes both sets work and distributes the work load.

- It provides a smoother pedalling movement that saves wasted energy.

During your first weeks of riding, you shouldn't feel any real need for straps and clips. You have too many other things to occupy your mind. As a beginner, I used to see experienced cyclists riding with straps and clips, and I used to envy them. But I really envied their overall ability. I just didn't want those straps on my feet.

Gradually, however, you reach a point where you begin to master the basics of riding a bicycle. You feel that you're ready for more advanced lessons, and you realize that you are going to need straps and clips if you expect to advance as a cyclist.

When having straps and clips installed on your bicycle, be sure that you mention your shoe size. The clips come in different sizes.

After the straps and clips are installed, notice how the straps are tightened and loosened. Loosen them enough so they don't even touch your shoe when you are riding.

RIDING WITH TOE CLIPS

Here's how to get into the toe clips. Straddle your bicycle. Push the left pedal straight down to 6 o'clock. You can see where the weight of the clips make the pedal hang down. Flip the pedal with the bottom of your shoe and slip your foot in. *Don't tighten the strap.*

Pull the pedal up to about 10 o'clock and push off. Make sure you have a good open space in front of you and no traffic nearby. Pedal several times to increase your speed and then coast. Push the left pedal down so that the right pedal is straight up. Now check ahead of you to make sure the road is clear. Then look down and flip the pedal back with your right foot and slip your right foot onto the pedal.

At first you may not manage to get your foot onto the pedal in time and will have to pedal some more in order to maintain your speed. But keep at it until you succeed. It's going to take a couple of weeks before your learn to do this smoothly.

You should ride at least two or three times with the straps completely loose, just to get used to their being there. Practice slipping your foot into the clips and taking it out while riding. This will help you become accustomed to taking your foot off the pedals. You have to move your foot backwards. It is one of those things that sounds obvious, but isn't. You've got to work on that backward movement until it becomes a natural reflex action.

On your first ride (with the straps loose), hold your foot and ankle rigid for a few hundred feet. The tip of your shoe should be fitted snugly into the small metal toe clips. Pull up on the toe clips with your toes while pushing down with the other foot. This way you can see some of the benefits of the device at once and will be more anxious to get to the point where you can really use it.

After two or three rides, tighten the straps somewhat until they touch the top of your foot lightly. Try this for a couple of rides. By then, you should be ready to make use of the straps and clips. Nevertheless, you still have one more step to think about.

Most riders keep their straps tight on long, open trips outside the city. But in city riding, with its many stops, they prefer to keep the straps loose. I found this to be good advice. When in the city, I keep the straps snug around my feet, but not too tight. It's only on long country rides that I tighten them up.

The reason I advise strapping your left foot down first and then your right foot is a simple one. Whenever I have to stop at a corner, I pull up, extract my right foot, and step on the curb. The left foot is not removed from the pedals. I estimate that in a normal ride, I remove my right foot from the pedal at least 25 times for every time I remove the left one.

Practice wriggling that right foot *out* of the straps. Don't wait until you have to. Do it while you are on a quiet road with no traffic.

Don't pull straight back, but move your heel to the left and pull and then to the right and pull. Once you get the hang of it, try to do it faster and faster. You never know when you will have to pull your foot out in an emergency.

Now, for the first time, you can really start pulling up with your whole foot instead of just with your toes against the toe clip. You can best appreciate the improvement by riding on a street with a slight uphill grade that you can really pull against. You'll notice, too, that very soon you'll be able to take grades and hills in a higher gear.

Snug is about as tight as you want the straps to be in city riding. Just how snug depends on how fast you can get your feet out of the straps. If you're having trouble, loosen the straps.

SADDLE, HANDLEBAR AND BRAKE LEVER ADJUSTMENTS

There are only three things to consider when adjusting your bicycle to fit your measurements. These are the saddle, the handlebars, and the brake levers.

Saddle. There are three possible adjustments you can make on the saddle: you can raise or lower it; you can tip it forward or backward; you can move it forward toward the handlebars or you can move it back.

● To adjust the saddle height, sit squarely on the saddle. Reach down with one foot and place your heel on the pedal while the pedal is at its lowest point. You should have just a slight bend in your knee. If you raise the saddle quite a bit, make sure that two or three inches of the seat post are still inserted in the seat tube. If necessary, get a longer seat post.

● The front of the saddle should be tipped just slightly upward. This may seem like an uncomfortable position, and it would be if you were always sitting erect. Just remember that you spend most of your time leaning forward.

● Find the proper distance from saddle to handlebars by placing the back of your elbow against the nose of the saddle. The tips of your fingers should just reach the handlebars. There are other factors such as your age and physical condition which may determine the precise saddle distance from the handlebars, but for now this "rule of elbow" should be sufficient.

If you should make these or any other adjustments, make

them one at a time. Taking each adjustment in succession will help you determine if you made them correctly. After you've made your adjustment, ride your bicycle for some distance to see if the adjustment you made is comfortable. This post-adjustment testing is a good method of helping you identify quickly any improper adjustment that causes discomfort. Otherwise, you would waste time over-adjusting the saddle.

Remember, don't make adjustments on your bicycle during your first few rides unless something is drastically wrong.

Handlebars. There are two adjustments that can be made on the handlebars: the angle of the bars and their distance above the frame. You can also move them forward or backward, but that is something you should do in the presence of the dealer or an experienced cyclist. Moving them forward or backward means you have to buy a different handlebar stem to attach them to. And you may also have to adjust the seat.

● Look at the top of the handlebars where the bars bend out toward the brake levers. The portion going out to the brake levers should be level. If it slopes down or up, you have to bend your wrists too much.

You can make this adjustment by looking at the bottom bars, and adjusting the bars so that the bottom bars are level or slope downward toward you at an angle of no more than 10 degrees.

● The top bar of the handlebars should be level with the top of the saddle. If you have to raise the bars, make sure enough of the stem is still inside the head tube. If you have less than about 2½ inches, you may have to buy a longer stem.

Brake Levers. There is no rule, method or system for adjusting brake levers. They should be moved only if you find it too difficult to use them in the position they were installed. Don't move the levers unless there is some definite advantage in doing so.

Never make an adjustment just for the sake of making an adjustment. Make it only to correct a problem.

If you purchased your bicycle from a reputable dealer, any breakdown or repairs should be his responsibility during the first few months. Any good dealer will request that you bring your bicycle back to the shop within 30 to 90 days for a complete, free checkup. Cables and chains stretch, screws can come loose, and parts need to be oiled on even the best bicycles.

Yet there are a few things that do require steady maintenance from the first day you purchase your bicycle, and you will have to learn to do them yourself. The first thing you will have to learn to do is to take care of the tires.

CLINCHER TIRES

Clincher tires are overwhelmingly more popular than sew-up tires. They have certain advantages which make them the tire most commonly used.

The clincher tires have wires imbedded into the lips of the tire. This provides sufficient rigidity to the tire so that it can grip the rim of the bicycle wheel in much the same manner as your automobile tires grip the rim of your car wheel.

The clincher is a heavier tire than the sew-up. It can weigh two or three times as much, which results in a number of advantages. It is a stronger tire than the sew-up. It is far less prone to flats and blowouts. While the cyclist using sew-ups may regard flat tires as a regular part of cycling, the cyclist using clinchers can, with a little care, consider flats as rare events.

In addition to the extra weight of the tire, the wheels used for clincher tires are heavier than those used for sew-up tires. The two types of tires are *not* interchangeable on the same wheel.

When you have a flat with a clincher tire while on the road, you can't replace the tube, or fix the flat on the spot. For someone in a hurry, it takes a lot longer to fix a flat on a clincher tire than it does to replace a sew-up tire with the spare one.

Although you can carry a spare clincher tire tube, you cannot carry a spare clincher tire. The clincher tire is rigid enough that it can't be folded into a neat package and carried along like a sew-up tire.

With any tire, you have two things to deal with: maintaining proper tire pressure and fixing flats.

Most tires have the proper air pressure marked on the tire. Clincher tires require only 65 to 90 pounds of air pressure.

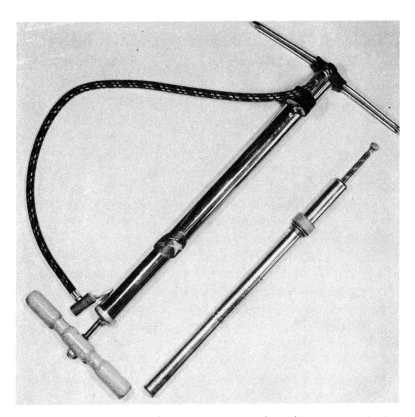

The regular foot pump (above) and the hand pump (below) have hoses and valves for clincher tires. You can also purchase sew-up hoses for these pumps.

Get a hand pump to carry along with you when riding and a foot pump to use at home. The foot pump is a lot easier to use. Also, purchase a gauge from your bicycle store. Don't make the mistake of going to a store and buying a regular auto tire gauge. They don't measure much above 40 pounds or so. Better yet, get a regular hand pump that has a gauge installed on it. It's more expensive, but the convenience is worth it.

Get into the habit of checking tire pressure before you leave home. It's a lot easier and you can avoid problems on the road. Don't "play it safe" by overfilling the tires. If the tire pressure is supposed to be 70 pounds, stop at 70 pounds. Tires can heat up on the road and the expanding air can cause a blowout.

Be careful with all bicycle tires when filling them at a gas station. It only takes a few seconds to blow out a tire. Fill the tire in very short bursts. Don't depend on the gauges attached to the air pump.

FIXING YOUR CLINCHER

If you are much over 40, fixing a flat clincher tire won't be that strange a task. You have either fixed flats on tires with inner tubes or else watched your father fix them. Follow this method to fix your clincher:

• First you need two items: a set of tire irons and a patch kit. Don't use a screwdriver and a pair of pliers to release the tire from the rim! A screwdriver makes an ideal tool for putting another hole in the tube. Tire irons consist of two or three small iron bars with bent tips, and are available at your local bike shop. The patch kit consists of patches, glue and a scraper.

• Turn the bicycle upside down. Before you do anything else, turn the wheel slowly, and see if you can find what caused the flat. If it's still there, you'll avoid the trouble of hunting for the hole by submerging the tube in a bucket of water.

• Mark the hole in some way. If the flat was a result of riding over broken glass, leave the piece of glass (or whatever) in the tire until you've taken the tire off. However, if you're afraid that it will cause additional punctures, remove it.

• Remove the wheel from the frame. (A flat can often be fixed while the wheel is still on the bicycle, but it's easier to handle it when you have the wheel off.) If you have to remove the rear tire, take a good look at how the chain goes over the rear derailleur. This examination will acquaint you with the rear derailleur, making it easier to replace the rear wheel.

• Slide the curved edge of one tire iron under the edge of the tire. Some tire irons have little slots which enable you to hook one of them to a spoke while you use the next one. Avoid damaging the spoke.

Use the next iron to work more of the tire over the rim until you can slip the tire loose by hand.

• Fill the tire up to a moderate pressure, and search for the hole by immersing the tire in water and looking for a stream of air bubbles.

• Dry the tire off before patching. Using the scraper, gently rub the area clean around the puncture without grating too deep. Remember, this isn't a thick automobile tire. Clean well around it. Now put cement around and over the hole. Make sure that the area you cover with cement is larger than the size of the patch you intend to use, or you'll have loose edges on the patch.

While the cement is drying, you can occupy your time by removing whatever caused the flat. Check the interior lining of the tire to make sure it is smooth. (If not, you can make a boot or protective pad of a larger patch which should at least last until you get home.) Let the cement dry until it is tacky. Remove the patch's protective coating, and apply the patch to the tube.

• Slip the tube inside the tire. Put the tube back on the rim by inserting the tube's valve through the rim first. Then work away from the valve, inserting the tube in two directions. Once you have the tube inside the tire, slip the edge of the tire back on the rim with the tire irons. Be careful not to pinch the tube with the tire irons.

• Fill the tire to a moderate pressure, then let the air out. (This gives the tire a chance to properly expand and remove folds and pinches.) Then inflate the tire.

There is one other point to remember. Occasionally a flat is caused by a protuding spoke that punctures the tube. So check the interior of the wheel every time for protruding spokes even when you know they weren't the cause of the flat.

Take the bicycle to the shop and have them show you how to file or nip off the edge of the protruding spoke. An experienced cyclist will tell you that doing this is simple. However, few things are simple the first time they're done.

SEW-UP TIRES

Sew-up tires are lighter. Tires for regular use are 10 to 15 ounces. Clincher tires and tubes from up to 30 ounces. Sew-up tires are smaller in diameter than clincher tires. With air pressures of 100 pounds and up, less of the tire touches the ground, making it easier to pedal. They are more responsive. In addition, sew-up tires are easy to change while on the road. They don't have the wires imbedded in the tire like the clincher tires, and spares can be carried folded up. An experienced rider can remove one sew-up and have another in its place in less than five minutes.

What are the disadvantages? Sew-up wheels are lighter and more prone to damage from bumps. As for the tires themselves, they have two major disadvantages. Being much lighter and thinner than clincher tires, they are far more likely to puncture. And while you can replace a sew-up tire much faster than you can fix a flat on a clincher tire, fixing a flat on a sew-up is a lot harder than fixing a flat on a clincher tire.

A sew-up tire's makeup is complicated. First you have the tube which is extremely light and thin. The tire is wrapped around the tube. A layer of cloth or tape is placed inside the tire to protect the tube from the tire where the edges of the tire meet. Then the two lips or edges of the tire are actually sewn together.

Another layer of cloth or tape is then glued over the part where the tube is sewn together. The finished product looks somewhat like a circular sausage. Glue is applied to the rim of the bicycle wheel and the tire when the tire is glued to the rim.

CHANGING YOUR SEW-UP TIRE

● Remove the wheel from the bicycle. Peel the tire off, beginning at the side away from the valve. Once you have it off, check the glue on the wheel. If it is somewhat sticky, it will generally hold the replacement tire at least until you can get home and remove the tire and apply more glue. However, the wheel must be cleaned regularly when changing tires to prevent glue build-up. Some people use an adhesive strip instead of glue. The strip, which is sticky on both sides, is wrapped around the rim.

● Always insert the valve in the rim first and start from that point, making sure the tire is on straight and doesn't twist and turn. Then all you have to do is inflate it.

• Use your emergency air pump for sew-up tires. However, you'll need a different air hose attachment. Be sure and ask for it when you buy a pump. In addition, sew-up valves (presta-valves) don't fit gas station air pumps. Buy a small attachment to screw on to the tire valve, then you can use a gas station pump.

PATCHING YOUR SEW-UP TIRE

• Once you have the tire off, pump it up and submert it in water. Don't be misled by bubbles escaping near the valve. Since the tire is sealed all the way around, some bubbles will always escape from the valve.

• When you have found the leak, mark the tire with chalk, and remove four to six inches of tape from the tire. Do this carefully, using a pair of pliers. Removing the tape from the area of the leak exposes the sewn threads that hold the edges of the tire together.

• Cut three to five inches of the thread where you have the puncture marked, by slipping a razor blade under the thread and pulling *away* so you don't cut the tire. Remove the cut threads. Now move aside the interior flap that you see inside the tire and pull enough of the tube out to look for the puncture.

• Now turn to your patch kit. A patch kit for sew-ups is different from one for clinchers. Because the tubes are thinner, the kit has fine sand paper for you to use instead of a grater. The patches are much thinner, and a needle, thread and a thimble are included. The kits I've seen all supply plastic thimbles. Get yourself a metal one. I was sewing a tire back once and the thimble cracked.

• Gently sandpaper the tube clean over the puncture, and apply the cement. When it becomes tacky, apply the patch after removing its protective cover.

• Sprinkle talcum powder on the tube, and re-insert it into the tire. Now sew the tire together without trying to imitate the fancy stitching. Just sew over and under so that the thread is sewn in a circular pattern. Don't miss any holes. Overlap the other thread and be careful not to puncture the tube. Now glue back the outer flap with some of the kit's glue.

● Check the wheel for accumulated glue. Clean the glue off before applying a new coat. Put the tire on, starting at the valve and working away from it. Make sure the tire is on straight.

Sew-up tires are more like a subtle refinement. They improve a rider's performance, however, the beginning rider is simply not good enough to take or appreciate the advantages of sew-up tires. The more fragile sew-ups and the more fragile wheels take more expert and more accurate riding than the new cyclist is capable of.

● Be careful when putting on the rear wheel. Center the wheel before you tighten it up, or it may end up rubbing against one of the rear chainstays. Occasionally the rear wheel may slip when riding, and the tire will rub abainst the chainstays. Just loosen the nuts holding the wheel, center it and tighten the nuts again.

MAINTENANCE CHECKS

Hang up your bicycle and spin the wheels. Make sure that the brake pads aren't brushing against the wheels. If just one is touching, tap the brakes gently on the opposite side. Generally, this will move the pad away from the wheel. Check the brake levers next. If you pull on a lever and it comes all the way down and touches the handlebars before the brakes lock, take your bicycle to the shop and have them tighten the brakes.

Now check your derailleurs. Make sure that the chain can be moved onto all 10 positions. The most common problem occurs when a rear derailleur won't move the chain onto the smallest or largest gear. Sometimes the derailleur moves too far, making the chain slip off the gears. The same thing can occur on the front derailleur when it won't move the chain from one gear to the other.

To correct these problems you must adjust the derailleur. First, determine the brand name and model of both front and rear derailleurs. Then go to a bookstore and look at the books on bicycle maintenance. Make sure that the book has an —with photographs—on adjusting the brand and model derailleur you have. Take the book home and set it up by your bicycle as you made the adjustments. You will have to make this adjustment sooner or later.

The first time I tried it (without a book), I spent two hours attempting the adjustment, and got everything so thoroughly out of whack that I had to take the bicycle back to the dealer. However, I began to understand how the adjustments should be made. Now they are just a matter of routine.

Accessories and Equipment

As long as you ride only in the practice area, all you need is a pump and a tire gauge. But once you begin venturing several miles away from home or your car, there are a number of things you will need.

ESSENTIAL EQUIPMENT

● Remember that there are two kinds of tires which are available for use on 10-speed bicycles, clinchers and sew-ups.

With clinchers, you'll need a set of tire irons to get the tire off the rim, and a patch kit. (These two can usually be purchased at a bicycle shop for a dollar or two.) Both tire irons and patch kit should be taken with you wherever you go. Usually the patch kit comes in a cardboard box. Discard the box as it takes up too much space.

If you have tubular or sew-up tires, you'll not need tire irons. Remember, the tire is glued to the wheel and is removed by deflating it, then peeling it off the rim.

Ask for a patch kit for sew-up tires. You can't use patches from a clincher tire patch kit to repair a sew-up tire which is punctured. Clincher tire patches are too thick.

If you have sew-ups, you need not take the patch kit with you on the road. Take a spare tire or two along on trips. Sew-up tires are flexible and can be folded and carried with you.

● Get a first aid kit that is complete, but small in volume. I found that the most common type of injury is a brush burn on the arm or leg. Quite often it is so large that none of the band-aids in the first aid kit is large enough to cover it. I always keep one or two 2- by 3-inch band-aids in the first aid kit. Get a box of small alcohol wipes to clean off scrapes and bruises. On the back of your first aid kit, glue a paper with your name and address along with the name of who to contact in case of an emergency.

● If you do intend to carry any tools at this point, a six-inch crescent wrench and a screwdriver should cover most of the repairs you're likely to be capable of doing. Purchase the kind of screwdriver where the stem and handle can be separated when not in use. The average screwdriver is usually too long to fit in the normal size carrier bag. Have one regular stem and one Phillips head stem.

● Under the back of most saddles there are two bars where you can attach a small carrier bag.

Never buy a carrier bag first. Go through this chapter, decide just what you intend to carry with you, buy those items and *then* buy the bag. That way, you can load the bag on the spot and make sure you have one that is large enough.

Straps for many of the bags can be purchased separately. So if a strap wears out on you, purchase just a strap. Don't go out and buy a new bag.

● You may be the kind of person who never leaves his bicycle unattended. But if you do, a lock and chain are essential. The proper way to lock your bicycle is to pass the chain through the spokes of the front wheel, wrapping the chain around and through the tubing in the frame and through the rear wheel. There are thieves who steal wheels only, especially if they are quick-release wheels.

If you need to lock your bicycle frequently, buy a carrier bag large enough to store the lock and chain. If you intend to lock or chain it up only rarely, perhaps you can carry the chain around waist, or wrap it around the stem just beneath the saddle.

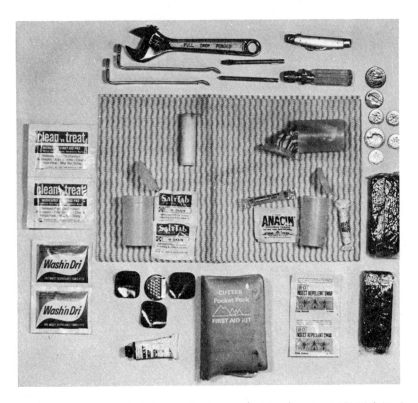

The above travelling kit includes two tire irons, screwdriver (regular and Phillip's head stem), pocket knife, two fruit bars, first aid kit, tire patches, insect repellent napkins and antiseptic napkins for cuts and bruises.

No chain and lock has yet been devised that can stop the experienced and well-equipped thief. The more expensive the bicycle, the more tempting a target it becomes. Therefore, where you park and lock your bicycle can be as important as locking and chaining it. Avoid isolated parking spots. Put your bicycle where the would-be thief has to operate in the open, in front of others. Since there is no foolproof way of really stopping the professional thief, try and make things as time consuming and as risky as possible for him.

● An emergency tire pump becomes an essential item as soon as you leave the practice area. The emergency tire pump looks like an aluminum tube. Get a good one which is both lightweight and sturdy. If your pump doesn't work while you are on the road, all your other preparations for repairing a flat have been wasted.

When you buy the emergency pump, you may not see an air line. Look at one end of the pump, and you'll see a small circular bronze fitting. Pull on it. That's the air line. Once you have it out, screw it onto the tire and then screw the pump onto the air line and pump.

The emergency air pump is not a replacement for the air pump you have at home. It is designed to pump enough air into a tire to permit you to get to the nearest gas station or your home where the tire can be inflated properly.

One additional point: most emergency pumps sold have a valve designed to fit clincher tires. If you have sew-up tires you'll

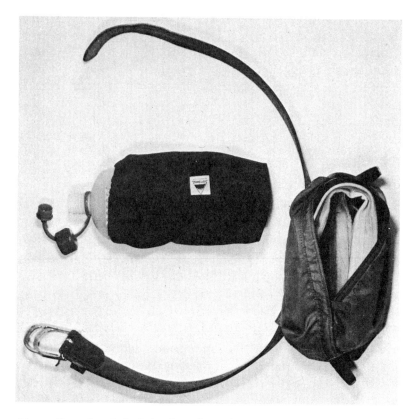

The small pouch and plastic bottle can be carried while you're not riding. The pouch on the right can carry a camera, lunch or a spare sew-up tire.

need a different air line. However, you can use the same pump.

Two small clips are sold with each air pump. These are attached to the bicycle frame. One word of caution. When installing these clips and the air pump, make sure you don't obstruct or impede any of the cables leading to the derailleurs or the brakes.

- Anyone who intends to ride a bicycle any distance or any length of time is going to need an available supply of water. This is especially true during the first weeks when you'll consume a lot of water while riding.

Water bottles come with a holder that attaches to your bicycle. There are two main kinds of holders. One kind attaches to the frame of your bicycle. The other attaches to the handlebars. The idea is to permit you to drink without stopping.

Many mountaineering and backpacking stores sell a small cloth pouch designed to carry a plastic water bottle up to a quart in size. The cloth pouch can be slipped on your belt and carried behind you like the old GI canteen. Later on, when you don't need the water bottle on your neighborhood travels, you still have a water bottle and a carrier that you can use on walks or hikes.

HELPFUL ACCESSORIES

- Salt tablets can be helpful for preventing muscle cramps when cycling in hot weather. They can be purchased by the bottle or in small packets containing two tablets to the packet.
- Moistened packaged napkins are the small paper napkins that are packaged individually in foil. They're useful for cleaning your hands after eating a roadside snack or just for cooling off your face. They also come in handy after you've had to fix the chain when it slips off the gears.
- Carry along one or two large, good quality paper napkins and a tiny plastic vial of borax cleanser. If your hands get really greasy you can clean them off with the borax and a touch of water from your water bottle. I prefer the better napkins because the average paper towel has a tendency to shred before you get your hands clean.

• Many backpacking stores sell small round plastic containers. They are inexpensive and light. The one I carry Borax in is about the same thickness as a slim fountain pen. The larger one is about the same diameter as the bicycle tire. There's always a few small things you want to take along. Using these containers with their snap-on covers you can keep everything in one place. For example, I can pack the following in the larger containers: patches for tires; scraper for tires; emergency five-dollar bill; 50 cents in change for emergency phone calls; four salt tablets; plastic bag.

There are other accessories available. Whether you use them or not is pretty much your decision.

• Horns and bells cost money and add weight to your bicycle. The human voice provides the same services and probably does it better.

• The law requires the cyclist riding at night to have lights: a front light that provides you with enough light to see and which is visible at least 300 feet in front of you, and a red rear reflector or a red rear light, which must be visible for 300 feet behind you.

I strongly advise you to stick to daytime riding your first 500 miles. Even now I won't ride at night. I've seen too many cyclists who ride at night have too many close shaves with automobiles.

The most common light is one that operates off a small generator run by a roller that rubs against the tire. The main problem with a generator light is that it doesn't operate when you are standing still at an intersection.

If you must ride at night, I suggest you purchase two battery-operated lights and attach them to the front and rear of your bicycle. You may also need a battery charger. Of course, the problem with batteries is that when they fail, you are left with no way to revive them on the road.

A popular light now available looks like a two-headed flashlight and attaches to the arm or leg. The idea is that the movement will attract the attention of car drivers. I didn't say it is a good light. I just said it was popular.

● Sooner or later, there will be occasions when you want to carry something along with you on your bicycle. There are several kinds of racks, baskets, and other carriers available for this purpose.

Handlebar baskets are usually medium size. Some are made of metal and others of straw or wicker. There are snap-on types available and others which may be permanently attached.

These are generally best for carrying small objects that are not too wide or too long. A heavy Sunday paper does not fit in one too well unless you can fold it.

There are two general kinds of rear wheel baskets. One kind fits on a small stand directly over the rear wheel. The other type is generally attached much like a carrier stand and consists of two baskets, one hanging on each side of the rear wheel. These are generally metal, although some of the over-the-rear-wheel baskets may be of lighter materials. These baskets are generally attached in a manner that makes it difficult for you to install them and should normally be considered as permanent installations.

Most baskets and carriers are heavy. They add weight to your bicycle. Loaded, they affect the steering and handling of the bicycle. This means that you have to learn two ways of handling your bicycle: one when the baskets are empty and the other when they are loaded.

A reasonable compromise is to get the small rear carrier. It will handle small objects and doesn't add too much to the bicycle's weight.

There is the small pouch, mentioned earlier, that carries a water bottle of up to a quart in size. It has the advantage of going with you when you leave your bicycle for a walk. However, if you're wearing clothing that doesn't have a belt, there is no way to carry it.

The water bottle pouch and small carrying bag are small enough and low enough that they will not affect riding or handling significantly. The knapsack and bicycle bag when loaded can raise your center of gravity and put an added strain on your back and arms.

No carrying case is perfect. It can only be a compromise. The beginning rider should carry as little as possible.

　　　　　　　　　　　　　　Serious Cycling for the Beginner

- Whether or not to use fenders depends pretty much on the climate where you intend to bicycle.
- Helmets are available for a cyclist's protection. If you are going for slow rides on quiet streets, perhaps you can do without one. If you are going to be doing high speed, downhill riding or riding in heavy traffic, you should use one. There are two basic kinds of helmets. The old style helmet is not really a helmet at all. It consists of a thick leather strap that goes around your head like a headband and a couple of leather strips that run over the top of your head from front to back. It is better than nothing, but provides only minimal protection.

The new bicycle rider's helmet is much lighter than a motorcycle helmet. In addition, it is vented. This venting is crucial. A motorcyclist just sits there while the motorcycle does the work. On the other hand, the cyclist can really build up a "good head of steam" when riding, and become overheated without proper ventilation.

I strongly recommend that you wear some kind of additional protective headgear when you ride in the sun. You may be able to get by at first without a hat or cap if your riding is restricted to short rides in the early morning or late afternoon. But as you gain experience, you'll one day find yourself out in the hot midday sun with a long ride ahead of you. That's when you are going to need protective headgear.

CLOTHING

For the beginning rider, any loose, short-sleeved shirt should be good enough. If you feel that you need some protection for your arms at first, you can try a long-sleeved shirt.

Once you get more involved in riding, you'll want close-fitting clothes that don't flap in the wind. Pullover T-shirts or polo shirts are generally sufficient if you get a good, close fit.

Later you'll find that the choice of a shirt becomes more complicated and is determined by the kind of shorts you wear. Many riding shorts don't have any pockets. The first time I wore riding shorts I realized why women carry purses. I was stuck with things to carry and no pockets to carry them in.

● The answer was the cyclist's riding shirt. Cycling shirts are generally multi-colored, composed of strips of different colored cloth. Generally, they are made of cotton or of nylon. The cotton shirt is quite comfortable and is only half the price of the nylon shirt.

The type that combines comfort with efficiency best is a pullover shirt with close fitting sleeves and neck. This shirt usually has five pockets, two in the front and three in back. The two front pockets are located right next to each other and are up high on the chest.

Eventually, if you ride enough, you may want to purchase cycling shorts. You might save time, money and trouble by going directly to them, instead of wearing long pants.

Riding shorts come in a variety of styles. One common style is made of 100 percent wool and is somewhat stretchable. There is no belt and the legs fit snugly to avoid their riding up.

The key part of riding shorts is the chamois lined crotch— an inner lining to prevent chafing on long rides.

Of course this means that if you want to utilize your chamois-lined shorts, you have to wear just them and nothing underneath. Wearing underclothing defeats the whole purpose of the chamois lining. You may spend the first few days feeling uncomfortable and having nightmares of your riding shorts splitting in the wrong place at the wrong time, but you'll soon get used to it.

● For the beginner and for the cyclist who will never take long rides, some type of tennis shoe should be sufficient. However, if you are really going to get involved in longer rides, you should consider buying cycling shoes.

Cycling shoes have a number of advantages. They are lightweight. The heel, for example, is almost non-existent since you don't need one for riding. The soles are made of thin leather. The top is usually light leather or some similar material. The pair I wear has holes drilled all over the top to provide cooler riding.

Tennis shoes are a good choice to begin with. Most of us have a pair and they are cheap. Riding shoes start off at $15 or so, and are designed specifically for cycling.

It is not always easy to find cycling shoes. If you cannot find any at your local bicycle shops, you can always get them from a mail order house that sells bicycle accessories. Before you order them, I suggest you go down to your local shoe store and get your exact foot measurements.

- The use of gloves while riding is often a personal matter. Whether or not you use them depends on how much you ride and the condition of your hands.

When I first began riding, I just didn't see any need for gloves. My rides were fairly short at the time, seldom taking more than two hours or being longer than 15 or 20 miles. Weeks went by and my hands felt fine.

Then, one Saturday morning, I took a 40-mile ride. I wasn't riding very hard, since I stopped occasionally and took over four hours for the trip. But by the time I got home, my hands felt like ground hamburger and were just about as red. On any ride much over 30 miles I find gloves a must. I don't recommend this distance for beginning cyclists. However, I strongly recommend that you wear gloves when you're capable of cycling 30 miles or more. If a five-mile ride gives you sore hands, buy gloves.

Cyclists in different parts of the country ride in all kinds of weather. If yours is a particularly cold climate, you will need a lot of cold weather gear. You undoubtedly know what you should wear, but you should keep the following guidelines in mind. You may have to compromise somewhat, but you need something to compromise.

- Try to wear clothing that is not too baggy or loose or that will flap in the breeze. Such clothing creates wind resistance and can get caught on parts of your bicycle. You'll soon realize that heavy clothing makes you feel less agile than light clothing. Heavy clothing weighs you down and inhibits your movements.

- Avoid wearing clothes which are too constricting. Why wear clothing that you have to fight against? This is where you may have to compromise by wearing clothing that is both close-fitting and yet lets you move freely.

- Wear the kind of clothing that permits you to take the outer layers off as you cycle. In other words, a shirt and jacket is better than a heavy underwear and shirt.

There is a two-piece riding set consisting of a close-fitting jacket and pants that are sold at some cycle shops. These outfits are primarily meant for use on chilly days; they don't provide much protection in really low temperatures.

In general, remember that the cyclist's clothing is designed to make cycling easier. It is designed to stay out of your way and to protect you.

Should you go out and buy a complete outfit during your first week of cycling? I don't recommend it.

Wait until the need for something arises before you buy it. You will understand and appreciate it more. If you don't feel a real need for a certain item of clothing, then don't buy it.

A Complete Cyclist

After awhile, you may begin to run out of places to ride. You can only take the same trip so many times. So check the bookstores. If you live in a fairly large metropolitan area, there are usually books available describing one-day rides in your area. Some books specialize in shorter rides, others in longer ones. A word of caution: don't go on the longer, harder rides without checking the route first, unless you are very familiar with it.

Take long trips on easy roads. In terms of mileage, a long trip is one that you find long and not one that I find long. Let me explain how such trips helped me.

I learned to ride reasonably well enough on the suburban streets of the San Fernando Valley in Los Angeles. I even took a couple of 25-mile trips. Despite all of this, I still wasn't wholly at ease while riding. There were occasions when I had to do things quickly, and I would get confused and do them poorly. I would even have close shaves with the traffic, due to wrong decisions or poor bicycle handling on my part. I was still having to think too much about what I did, instead of making the right move automatically.

I live on one end of the San Fernando Valley and it's a little over 20 miles to the other side from my house. I selected two straight streets that ran parallel to each other for my next trip. Both streets began near my home and ran straight across the valley to the other side. Although they ran parallel to each other, they were a couple of miles apart.

I didn't really know if I could cycle 45 miles. I had never done more than 25 miles in one day. However, I felt that if I started getting tired, I could always turn around and come back. In addition, they were streets my wife was familiar with. If I really burnt out, she would have no trouble finding me if she had to drive out and rescue me.

The road surface was excellent. There were no difficult stretches, no surprises on the route. It was just straight out and straight back.

I began early on a Saturday morning when the traffic was light. The road went through the heart of the valley. It had a lot of red lights. (Certainly over 50, perhaps more.) The road back ran parallel to a railroad track so the red lights were six to 10 blocks apart.

Because I left early, I wasn't suddenly thrown into heavy traffic. The slow building of traffic was a lot easier to accept.

The ride taught me to "play" the red lights. By looking ahead, I learned to slow down or speed up and arrive at an intersection while the light was green. It helped me get used to the slower speed of a bicycle. If you are a block away from a signal and it turns green, perhaps you can speed up a little and make it in a car. But you can't do it on a bicycle unless it's a very short block.

I got accustomed to pulling over to the curb and stopping at many intersections, to watching for drainage grates and for cars making right turns, and to stopping at intersection curbs with my left pedal pointing down to avoid scraping my right pedal against the curb.

It was on these long but relatively simple trips that I really began to establish a cadence for myself.

I also learned one of the most important things about gears. It was here that I learned that the expert cyclist is not one who rides everywhere in 10th or high gear. He is the one who always rides in the *proper* gear.

When I took the first of these long trips, I still believed that one of the ways to improve your riding ability was to keep riding in a higher gear.

Following this misconception, I started off my first long trip one gear too high. That wasn't a major error, however it was an error. As a result, I began to run out of gas about 10 miles from home. I had to travel those last miles one gear too low and I had to stop and rest every couple of miles.

I took a similar trip the next weekend. This time I used the proper gear from the beginning. It was a breeze all the way.

Take long simple trips to improve your technique. Do they have to be 45 or 50 miles? Certainly not, but they should be trips that extend your cycling range at the same time they help you polish up your basic skills.

The complete cyclist may be one who can go fast and far, can ride in city traffic, on country roads, up and down hills, etc. But before you can become the complete cyclist, you have to master the basic skills. The skills you improve on long, straight trips are the basic ones.

After three or four such long trips, you won't need anyone to give you much advice. By then, you'll have a pretty good idea of what you can do.

There is one enjoyable moment that comes to all of us. After some long and difficult ride, you will suddenly look back in wonder and amusement at those days only a few short months before when you had difficulty making 20 trips around the parking lot. And you'll remember the day you actually did 10 whole miles and how proud you felt. You have a moment of real and deep satisfaction at how much you have accomplished since then.

So what is an expert cyclist? An expert cyclist is one who can do just about anything with a bicycle that any other cyclist his or her age can do. The key word is "age." If you are 50, you probably won't be able to do what a rider of 25 can do. Nevertheless, the expert cyclist of any age can do a remarkable number of things. Many riders in their 60s can ride a hundred miles a day. Riders in their 70s and 80s have done it.

The expert rider is one who can ride long distances and is capable of touring, high-speed riding and mountain riding. The expert may not be good at all of these, but is very good at those which he or she finds interesting. The expert can also do quite a bit of the maintenance, adjustment and repair work on his bicycle.

How long does it take? That depends on you. I doubt that

many people who work and can only ride in their spare time can make it in one summer. There is just too much to learn. The hardest parts are not those your brain must learn, but the things your whole body must learn.

If you plan to become an expert rider, then work hard at becoming a very good rider the first summer. Keep in shape during the winter by riding as often as the weather permits. You may achieve your goal by the end of the second summer.

Practice riding until you learn to do most things by reflex. If you have to stop and think about every single thing you do, you'll never become a first rate rider. A good rider does more things by reflex than by thinking each step.

If you can reach a point where you ride 10 or 15 miles at one time, you have done 90 per cent of the things you need to do to make a 40-mile trip. It's much harder to go from your first day of riding to 15-mile trips than it is to go from a 15-mile trip to a 40-mile one. So don't stop on the threshold. It's truly amazing how much you can see and enjoy on a trip of 25 to 50 miles. I've seen more in one day from the seat of a bicycle than I've seen in 500 miles from inside a car.

Unless you should turn to something like racing, camping or touring, there isn't too much else that you need to learn. During your next 1,000 miles of riding you will be refining what you have already learned. You will also grow stronger. Go out tomorrow or this weekend and ride up some difficult hills. Don't go back for a couple of months. When you finally do ride them again, you'll be pleasantly surprised at how much smaller and easier they have become.

There will be the joy of feeling really fit again. For many like myself, it will be the first time in years.

Equally important will be the feeling that you have tackled a difficult task and mastered it. Most of us get satisfaction from being able to do something well.

You have done the work of learning. Now enjoy it.

If you prefer being a loner who takes long rides alone on level streets or on steep hills, then do it. If all you want to do is ride around your own block 25 times, then do that.

If you like riding with others, pick a riding club that meets *your* needs. Don't change your style to meet their rules.

Clubs range from those whose riders line up single file and ride furiously for 50 miles without stopping or looking up the whole trip, to clubs whose members get on their bicycles, ride three miles to the beach or park and spend the day socializing before returning home. Find the one that suits you.

NOTES

NOTES